PROMOTING SOCIAL BONDS FOR IMPACT INVESTMENTS IN ASIA

MAY 2021

ASIAN DEVELOPMENT BANK

ADB

© 2021 Asian Development Bank
6 ADB Avenue, Mandaluyong City, 1550 Metro Manila, Philippines
Tel +63 2 8632 4444; Fax +63 2 8636 2444
www.adb.org

Some rights reserved. Published in 2021.

ISBN 978-92-9262-858-1 (print), 978-92-9262-859-8 (electronic), 978-92-9262-860-4 (ebook)
Publication Stock No. SPR210180-2
DOI: http://dx.doi.org/10.22617/SPR210180-2

The views expressed in this publication are those of the authors and do not necessarily reflect the views and policies of the Asian Development Bank (ADB) or its Board of Governors or the governments they represent.

ADB does not guarantee the accuracy of the data included in this publication and accepts no responsibility for any consequence of their use. The mention of specific companies or products of manufacturers does not imply that they are endorsed or recommended by ADB in preference to others of a similar nature that are not mentioned.

By making any designation of or reference to a particular territory or geographic area, or by using the term "country" in this document, ADB does not intend to make any judgments as to the legal or other status of any territory or area.

Please contact pubsmarketing@adb.org if you have questions or comments with respect to content, or if you wish to obtain copyright permission for your intended use that does not fall within these terms, or for permission to use the ADB logo.

Corrigenda to ADB publications may be found at http://www.adb.org/publications/corrigenda.

Note:
In this publication, "$" refers to United States dollars.

Cover design by Francis Manio.

Contents

Tables, Figures, and Boxes

Boxes

Foreword

The Asian Development Bank (ADB) is working closely with its developing member countries to tackle the coronavirus disease and mitigate its impact on developing Asia. The pandemic not only caused the first annual contraction in the region's economy in 6 decades, but it also poses serious and unique challenges to vulnerable groups. The pandemic highlights the importance of investments that generate social impacts to "build back better" and which pave the way for a sustainable recovery that is resilient under future shocks.

Social bonds have attracted growing attention in both Asia and around the world during the pandemic. Therefore, it is useful to understand the potential future allocation of capital that can contribute to sustainable development. This report presents a novel review of existing social bond markets in Asia and the world, focusing on their current impacts as well as desirable potential impacts in the future. This report was produced under an ADB technical assistance program that promotes knowledge about financing investments with positive social impacts, raises awareness and interest in social bonds, and ultimately contributes to the development of social bond markets in developing Asia.

We are delighted to share this review of how social bond markets can have important impacts in Asia and the Pacific. The report first describes the current profile of global and Asian social bond markets in terms of the social sectors that they address. A central part of the report identifies existing social challenges faced by developing Asia economies and how financial solutions such as social bonds can address them. The report further discusses existing impact measurements and management practices in social bond markets.

A key constraint to social bond market development is the lack of consistent standards and sound data collection, in addition to the lack of a standardized practical analytical framework and methodology to measure impacts. Compared to green finance, social finance seeks to tackle a wider range of issues. It is thus important for policy makers to support the development of common standards of information disclosure and impact measurement. Well-functioning social bond markets can help mobilize more resources to meet the region's funding needs in order to attain the United Nations Sustainable Development Goals and transition to sustainable development that benefits all Asians.

The study was prepared by Jane Hughes and Jason Mortimer under the direction of a team in ADB's Economic Research and Regional Cooperation Department, led by Shu Tian and supported by Donghyun Park, Kosintr Puongsophol, and Satoru Yamadera. We hope that this report will be useful for policy makers, issuers, and investors in their efforts to align the social bond market with the UN Sustainable Development Goals and maximize the social impact of social bonds in developing Asia.

Yasuyuki Sawada
Chief Economist and Director General
Economic Research and Regional Cooperation Department
Asian Development Bank

Acknowledgments

We would like to acknowledge the Asian Development Bank team for their generous help and support throughout this project: Shu Tian, Donghyun Park, Satoru Yamadera, Kosintr Puongsophol, and Mai Lin C. Villaruel. We would also like to thank Madeline Dixon for her excellent research assistance and David Ng of Cornell University and Sung Su Kim of the Asian Development Bank for their comments. Participants in the online workshop to prepare the report held on 5 November 2020 provided additional feedback and information that was very helpful, and we would like to acknowledge their support as well: Cedric Rimaud, Gempaku Okuyama, and Gladys Chua.

United Nations Sustainable Development Goals

1. No Poverty
2. Zero Hunger
3. Good Health and Well-Being
4. Quality Education
5. Gender Equality
6. Clean Water and Sanitation
7. Affordable and Clean Energy
8. Decent Work and Economic Growth
9. Industry, Innovation and Infrastructure
10. Reduced Inequalities
11. Sustainable Cities and Communities
12. Responsible Consumption and Production
13. Climate Action
14. Life Below Water
15. Life on Land
16. Peace, Justice and Strong Institutions
17. Partnerships for the Goals

Abbreviations

DIB	development impact bond
ESCAP	Economic and Social Commission for Asia and the Pacific
ESG	environmental, social, and governance
EUR	euro
GDP	gross domestic product
ICMA	International Capital Market Association
JPY	Japanese yen
MSMEs	micro, small, and medium-sized enterprises
OECD	Organisation for Economic Co-operation and Development
SBP	Social Bond Principles
SDG	Sustainable Development Goal
SIB	social impact bond
SMEs	small and medium-sized enterprises
SLB	sustainability-linked bond
UN	United Nations
UNCTAD	UN Conference on Trade and Development
UNESCO	United Nations Educational, Scientific and Cultural Organization
UNICEF	United Nations Children's Fund
US	United States

Executive Summary

The coronavirus disease (COVID-19) pandemic has magnified the effects of underlying social issues such as poverty and inequality, which highlights the need to build back better. With fast expansion of social bond issuance in 2020 globally and in Asia, it is important to understand how to optimize the use of social bonds to address urgent and relevant social issues in developing Asia and how to maximize their social impacts.* This report explores the relevant social issues that social bonds can be used to address, both in the short- and long-term.

Along with considerable growth in social bond issuance in 2020, there was also a significant change in social bonds' impact areas, most notably a shift from a prior focus on affordable housing to more pandemic-related project types such as education and training (including unemployment support), and socioeconomic crisis alleviation. In Asia, social bond issuance has typically focused on socioeconomic areas such as small and medium-sized enterprise (SME) finance, and transport access, representing 37% and 21%, respectively, of allocated social bond issuance from 2017 to 2020.

The COVID-19 pandemic has highlighted a few key areas that social bonds can address in developing Asia. A top priority area for social bond financing is a resilient and equitable health-care system. The pandemic has exposed the weaknesses, inequities, and shortages associated with health care in many developing economies. The COVID-19 crisis has also exposed vulnerabilities in food and water systems by straining supplies, disrupting food chains, and increasing food insecurity for millions of people. Frequent handwashing and proper sanitation are among the most effective measures in containing COVID-19.

Social bonds that support SMEs can help get both businesses and people back on their feet again after the economic shock of the pandemic and lockdowns. Even before the pandemic, SMEs faced numerous obstacles, particularly their lack of access to finance. Nearly all Asian (excluding high-income economies) social bond issuance in 2020 was allocated to SME financing, an understandable outcome given the nature of the shock and the economic structure of the region.

The pandemic has had a pernicious impact on educational opportunities in developing economies and has widened the education gap. Social bonds can channel funding to build schools and hire teachers. In particular, girls' education is one of the most effective ways to drive sustainable development, improve health, reduce conflict, and save lives. The pandemic has made a difficult situation worse, as girls who were forced out of school by the pandemic are much less likely than boys to return to their studies.

Social bonds can help advance gender equity. The pandemic has had a dramatically gender-differentiated impact throughout Asia and the Pacific. Social bonds could be used to reduce gender inequity and empower women by improving working conditions for female employees, decreasing the digital divide between men

---

* Social bonds are fixed-income instruments that raise funds for new and existing projects with positive social outcomes. Voluntary process guidelines for these bonds are set forth by the International Capital Market Association's Social Bond Principles, which provide guidance on the use of proceeds and target populations.

and women, and providing capital for underfunded women-owned SMEs. The pandemic also highlights the importance of other key areas such as building resilience to natural disasters, reducing the digital divide and poverty, and improving social protection. Social bonds can provide funding to strengthen these areas.

Impact measurement is central to the development of a well-functioning social bond market. The market lacks a commonly acknowledged set of practices to disclose information and define social impact measurement. Experimentation and innovation has been ongoing as market participants respond to rising demand from investors for impact investments, but there is as yet no widespread agreement on a single model of social impact assessment. The International Capital Market Association recommends that issuers track and report qualitative performance indicators as well as quantitative metrics. As investors link their portfolios comprehensively and quantitatively to the United Nations Sustainable Development Goals and communicate these efforts in a clear and standardized way to clients, it is also becoming more common for issuers to map their bonds' use of proceeds to individual Sustainable Development Goals.

It is challenging for policy makers, issuers, and investors to make investment decisions and plan resource allocation without data and standardized impact measurement methods. The good news is that impact measurement is improving with more efforts made on information disclosure and emerging standardization. From resilience to SME support, and gender equity to health care, social bonds will be a useful tool for financing the work needed for developing Asia to build back better.

Introduction—The Range of Social Impacts Addressed by Social Bonds

1

With social bond issuance setting a new record in 2020, it is important to explore how best to use these financial instruments going forward, specifically, which social issues to address and how to maximize deep and lasting impact.[1] The coronavirus disease (COVID-19) pandemic has disproportionately harmed poor, underserved, and vulnerable communities. COVID-19-linked and other social bonds have been deployed to address a variety of impact areas, and these bonds have been well received by investors.

But does social bond financing actually address social challenges that Asians face? Which social impact areas should issuers in developing Asia focus on more in their social bond issuances?[2] How should developing Asian economies prioritize these areas? Should issuers and policy makers first address low-hanging fruit or focus on complex and challenging problems?

This report addresses these questions by analyzing the impact areas that have been addressed by the social bond market to date and by introducing the impact measurement techniques that are currently in use and under development. It is important that developing Asia gets this right: that social bonds are used to "build back better" and not for minimally impactful projects or, worse, for "social washing" (i.e., claiming more social impact than projects can actually achieve).

Build Back Better

The COVID-19 pandemic is more than just a health crisis; it affects virtually all aspects of human development. It has magnified the effects of poverty and inequality, and led to greater suffering among vulnerable communities than the better-off. According to the United Nations Economic and Social Commission for Asia and the Pacific (UNESCAP), 40% of the population of Asia and the Pacific lacks access to health care, and 60% lacks access to adequate social protection. This reflects a number of underlying social issues, including unequal access to health care, education, food security, nutrition, social protection, and clean water.

These underlying difficulties and inequities highlight the need to build back better. As the United Nations (UN) notes: "The road to recovery offers countries the opportunity to improve their overall long-term sustainability and resilience, if planning starts now."[3] Recovery work can be viewed as two-pronged: (i) meeting short-term needs such as employment generation and health-care provision, and (ii) launching longer-term public works programs to reduce poverty and develop resilience to future disasters. Innovative financial instruments like social bonds can be used to strengthen infrastructure and resilience, and to reduce inequality through improved access to education, health care, and a social safety net. The build-back-better theme

---

[1] Social bonds are fixed-income instruments that raise funds for new and existing projects with positive social outcomes. Voluntary process guidelines for these bonds are set forth by the International Capital Markets Association's Social Bond Principles, which provide guidance on the use of proceeds and target populations.

[2] Developing Asia comprises the 46 developing member countries of the Asian Development Bank.

[3] UN Office for Disaster Risk Reduction. 2020. *Transformational Potential of COVID-19 Recovery in Asia.* https://reliefweb.int/report/world/transformational-potential-COVID-19-recovery-asia-pacific.

offers the possibility of financial returns from investments that are designed to align with the UN Sustainable Development Goals (SDGs).

Impact Areas Addressed to Date

From 2017 to 2020, the equivalent of more than $190 billion of publicly listed social bonds in total were issued that were compliant with the Social Bond Principles (SBP) of the International Capital Market Association (ICMA), with the annual issuance of social bonds increasing over eightfold from 2019 to 2020. We have calculated the estimated funding allocations to each of the ICMA's non-exhaustive list of designated social bond project categories and underlying project types, based on our review of the issuers' social or sustainability bond frameworks, and analysis of second-party opinions (Table 1). Based on these data, we find that the top project types by funding amounts from 2017 to 2020 were as follows: alleviation of crisis-related unemployment—typically through unemployment insurance and support measures ($65.6 billion or 34%); education and training ($31.4 billion or 16%); affordable housing ($29.8 billion or 16%); and micro, small, and medium-sized enterprise (MSME) finance ($24.6 billion or 13%). Of 2020's full-year issuance total, we estimate that health-related project allocations were only $18.7 billion, or 10% of the cumulative total (Figure 1).

Table 1: Classification of International Capital Market Association Social Bond Use of Proceeds by Project Category and Project Type

Project Category	Project Type	Most Commonly Targeted Population	Most Commonly Referenced SDG
Affordable Basic Infrastructure	Water and Sanitation	General Public	SDG 6—Clean Water and Sanitation
	Transport Infrastructure	General Public	SDG 11—Sustainable Cities and Communities
Affordable Housing	Affordable Housing	Low Income	SDG 11—Sustainable Cities and Communities
Access to Essential Services	Health	Elderly	SDG 3—Good Health and Well-Being
	Education and Training	Low Income	SDG 4—Quality Education
	Digital Access	Underserved	SDG 9—Industry, Innovation and Infrastructure
	Financial Services	Low Income	SDG 8—Decent Work and Economic Growth
Food Security and Sustainability	Food Security	Low Income	SDG 2—Zero Hunger
Employment Generation	SME Finance	MSMEs	SDG 8—Decent Work and Economic Growth
	Alleviation of Crisis-Related Unemployment	Crisis Affected	SDG 8—Decent Work and Economic Growth
Socioeconomic Advancement and Empowerment	Access and Opportunity	Low Income	SDG 8—Decent Work and Economic Growth
	Participation and Integration	Low Income	SDG 8—Decent Work and Economic Growth

MSMEs = micro, small, and medium-sized enterprises; SDG = Sustainable Development Goal.

Note: "Most Commonly Targeted Population" and "Most Commonly Referenced SDG" refer to the population type and SDG, respectively, found most frequently in social bond frameworks with use of proceeds allocated to a particular International Capital Market Association project type (nonexclusive).

Sources: International Capital Market Association. 2020. Social Bond Principles June 2020 Revision Use of Proceeds Project Category List (non-exhaustive). https://www.icmagroup.org/assets/documents/Regulatory/Green-Bonds/June-2020/Social-Bond-PrinciplesJune-2020-090620.pdf (accessed 3 March 2021); Authors' calculations based on text-mining and review of 126 extant issuer social bond frameworks and reviewer second opinions at the end of 2020.

Figure 1: Share of Global ICMA-Compliant Social Bond Issuance by SBP Project Type, 2017–2020 (USD-equivalent notional, estimated)

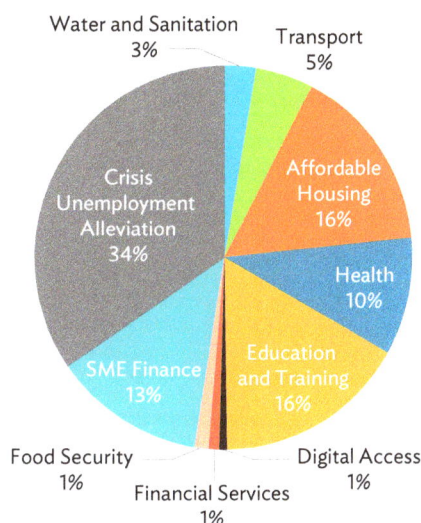

ICMA = International Capital Market Association, SBP = Social Bond Principles, SMEs = small and medium-sized enterprises, USD = United States dollar.
Sources: Authors' calculations based on review of Bloomberg data, issuer social bond frameworks, and reviewer Second Party Opinions.

These data demonstrate a significant change in the share of funds allocated to different social bond impact areas in 2020 (Figure 2). Allocated social bond financing shifted away from an initial focus on affordable housing to more pandemic-related project types such as education and training (including retraining support for unemployed workers), and alleviation measures for socioeconomic crisis-related unemployment (a new SBP project type in 2020) including funding for unemployment insurance at the national level. While global social bond issuance allocated to health in 2020 reached $14.8 billion equivalent from only $2.5 billion in 2019, this project type's share to total issuance remained relatively low at 10% and has not grown as a proportion of overall social bond issuance even during the COVID-19 pandemic. The relatively low share of health-allocated social bond issuance is somewhat surprising: our text-reference review based on all social bond frameworks for issuers in our database (including SBP-aligned projects under a sustainability bond frameworks, where applicable) indicates that 35% of all social bond frameworks directly address health, and 42% target SDG 3 (Good Health and Well-Being) (Figure 3). The implication of this divergence is that health-focused social bond issuance has strong potential for further growth since a relatively high proportion of social bond frameworks already include health-related projects as a target area for financing.

We find that the estimated allocations to various SBP project types show regional differences, particularly between Asian and non-Asian economies. For example, social bond issuance in Asia tends to focus on economic issues such as SME finance and transport infrastructure, representing 37% and 21%, respectively, of the region's allocated social bond issuance in United States (US) dollar notional terms from 2017 to 2020. ICMA-compliant social bond issuance in Asia during the review period came almost entirely from high-income economies, with Japan, the Republic of Korea, and Australia together representing 94% of the regional total from 2017 to 2020. For non-Asian economies (88% of issuers in this grouping come from high-income economies in Europe), the most prominent project types are education and training (25%), and affordable housing (24%), reflecting different priorities across regions.

Figure 2: Global ICMA-Compliant Social Bond Issuance by Year and SBP Project Type, 2017–2020 (USD-equivalent notional, estimated)

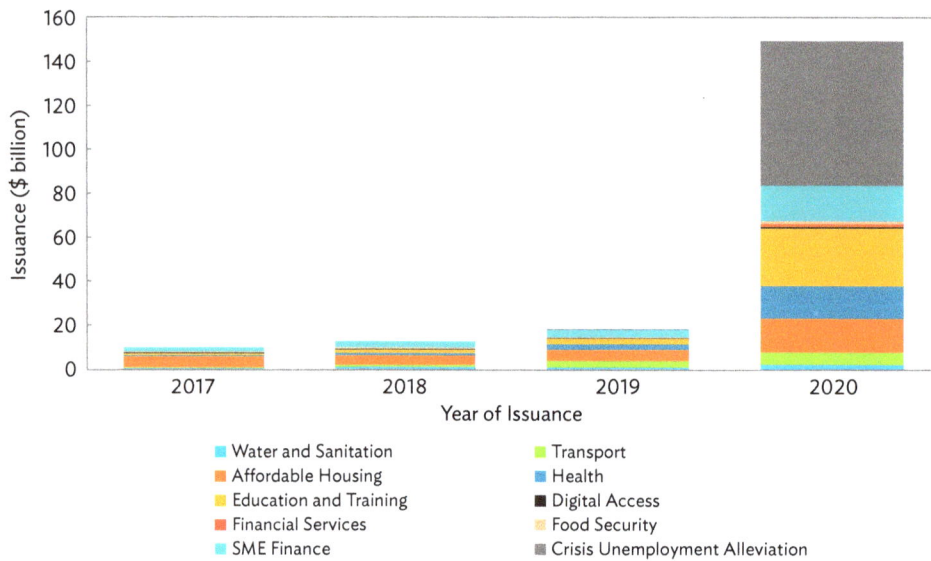

Legend:
- Water and Sanitation
- Affordable Housing
- Education and Training
- Financial Services
- SME Finance
- Transport
- Health
- Digital Access
- Food Security
- Crisis Unemployment Alleviation

ICMA = International Capital Market Association, SBP = Social Bond Principles, SMEs = small and medium-sized enterprises, USD = United States dollar.

Sources: Authors' calculations based on review of Bloomberg data, issuer social bond frameworks, and reviewer Second Party Opinions.

Figure 3: Share of Issuer Social (and Sustainability) Bond Frameworks That Reference SBP Project Categories and Types, Issued from 2017 to 2020

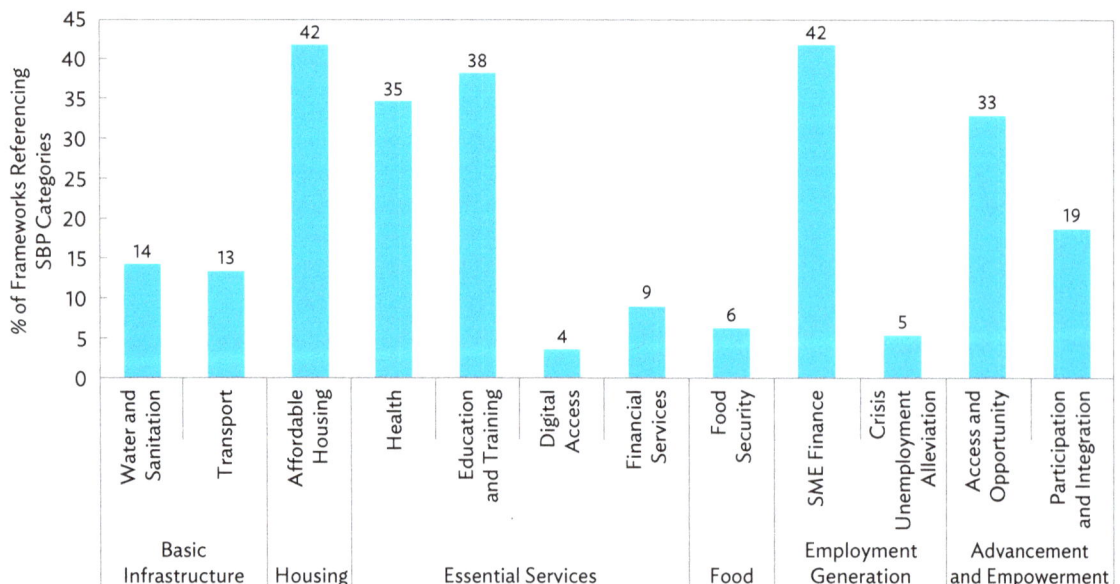

SBP = Social Bond Principles, SMEs = small and medium-sized enterprises.

Note: Percentages are based on the count of framework text references, not the United States dollar equivalent notional amount.

Sources: Authors' calculations based on review of Bloomberg data, issuer social bond frameworks, and reviewer Second Party Opinions.

Supranational and multinational issuers that by their remit allocate primarily to lower-income economies around the world, display a more balanced portfolio approach, with estimated allocations to SME finance (23%), education and training (20%), and affordable housing (11%) rounding out the top three SBP project types (Figure 4).

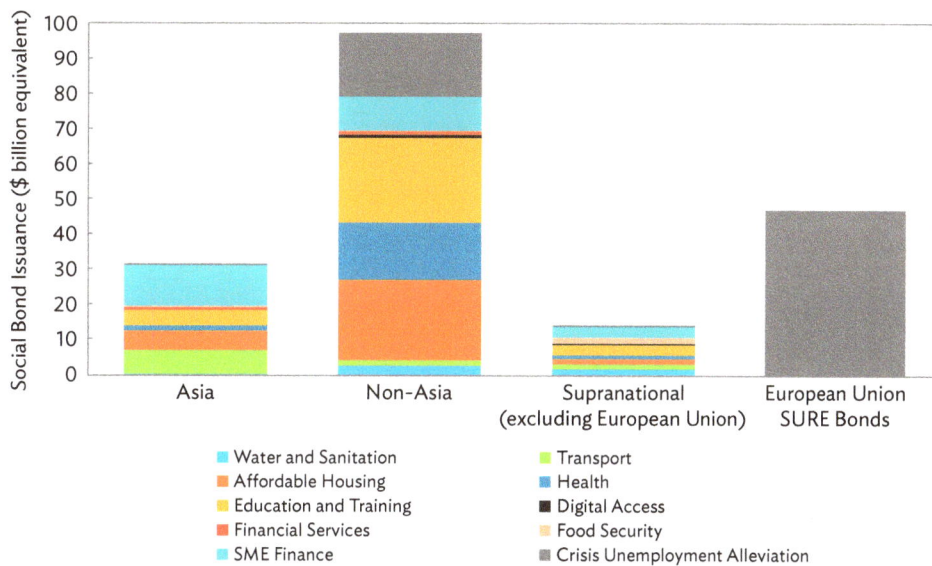

Figure 4: Cumulative Amount of ICMA-Compliant Social Bond Issuance by Estimated SBP Project Type Allocation and Region, 2017–2020 (USD-equivalent notional, estimated)

EU = European Union, ICMA = International Capital Market Association, SBP = Social Bond Principles, SMEs = small and medium-sized enterprises, SURE = Support to Mitigate Unemployment Risks in an Emergency, USD = United States dollar.

Notes: The "supranational" issuer group is broken down to show social bonds issued by the European Union under the Support to Mitigate Unemployment Risks in an Emergency program separately. In some cases for non-supranational social bond issuers with an official development assistance focus, the actual areas where projects take place may not match the country of issuance. However, for this report we assume that proceeds are applied to the country of the issuer's ultimate parent. Percentages in the figure represent the share of the United States dollar equivalent (notional, estimated) total.

Sources: Authors' calculations based on review of Bloomberg data, issuer social bond frameworks, and reviewer second opinions.

Given the nature of the COVID-19 crisis, it is surprising that more social bonds have not focused on health care as an impact area (Figure 4). However, the effects of the pandemic have cut across sectors, with impacts on virtually all aspects of human development, from education to inequality. Thus, social bonds may be used to productively address a wide variety of impact areas, including through bank-intermediated lending and project financing (Box 1). The following section of this report explores these impact areas, based on the project categories and types presented by the ICMA SBP, with a few additions. Table 2 briefly lists the impact areas to be addressed in the following section.

Box 1: Case Study—Chugoku Bank Social Bond for Socioeconomic Crisis Alleviation

In September 2020, Chugoku Bank (a regional lender in Japan) issued a social bond for supporting bank customers and borrowers affected by the coronavirus disease (COVID-19) pandemic. The bond raised funds for loans including emergency special loans for individuals, capital loans to corporate customers who were temporarily struggling due to the pandemic, and other loans related to mitigating the economic impact of the COVID-19 shock.

Chugoku Bank described its targeted impact as twofold: (i) the direct impact of stabilizing customers' cash flow and strengthening their financial base; and (ii) the indirect impact of maintaining companies' business and employment levels, and restoring regional economic stability for the medium- to long-term. The bond was linked to Sustainable Development Goal 8: promote sustained, inclusive, and sustainable economic growth; full and productive employment; and decent work for all.

The impact metrics for the bond are total loans outstanding and the number of eligible loans.

Source: Rating & Investment Information, Inc. 2020. *Chugoku Bank Social Bond Framework.* https://www.r-i.co.jp/news_release_sof/2020/08/news_release_sof_20200831_jpn_05.pdf [in Japanese].

Table 2: Possible Impact Areas to Be Addressed by Social Bonds

Impact Area	SDG Linkages	Case Study
Socioeconomic Crisis Alleviation	SDG 1, 3, 5, 6, 8, 9, 10	Chugoku Bank
Health, Water, and Sanitation	SDG 3, 6	SFIL Group Nipro Corporation
Food Security	SDG 1, 2, 3	African Development Bank
SME Finance	SDG 1, 5, 8, 9, 10	Bank of the Philippine Islands
Resilience	SDG 1, 2, 3, 6, 8, 11, 13	East Nippon Expressway Co. Ltd.
Education and Training	SDG 1, 4, 5, 8, 9, 10	Unedic
Girls' Education	SDG 1, 4, 5, 10	Rajasthan, India
Gender Equity	SDG 1, 5, 8, 10	Bank of Ayudhya (Krungsri)
Digital Inclusion	SDG 3, 4, 5, 8,	Credit Agricole
Poverty and Inequality	SDG 1, 4, 5, 8, 10	Region Wallonne Belgium

SDG = Sustainable Development Goal, SMEs = small and medium-sized enterprises.
Source: Authors' compilation.

Social Impacts Relevant to Developing Asia

2

Socioeconomic Crisis Alleviation
(SDG Linkages: SDG 1, 3, 5, 6, 8, 9, 10)

The COVID-19 pandemic has highlighted the need for increased investment in public health services and medical equipment, which will continue to be sizable, especially as populations age. This is necessary to both mitigate the impact of the COVID crisis, and to improve health-care services to prevent future such crises. At the same time, a number of hard-hit economies in developing Asia are already facing high and potentially unsustainable budget deficits that may crowd out such social spending.

The combination of rising expenditures to combat COVID-19 and increasingly unmanageable government budget deficits makes a compelling case for the greater use of social bonds. By raising money from private investors to directly address social needs, social bonds can direct capital to providing health-care services for vulnerable and underserved populations. Furthermore, these bonds may be used to finance COVID-19-linked social projects including

(i)   research and development of COVID-19 tests, vaccines, and medications;
(ii)   manufacturing and/or modification of existing machines to produce health safety equipment and hygiene supplies;
(iii) vaccine procurement and vaccination-related infrastructure and investments, including vaccine delivery services (e.g., cold chain storage and transport) and vaccine distribution (e.g., frontline workers); and
(iv)   increased health-care capacity for COVID-19 patients.

Health, Water, and Sanitation
(SDG Linkages: SDG 3, 6)

Medium- to longer-term health-care needs are another target issue area for social bond financing. As Figure 5 indicates, health-care spending per capita in much of developing Asia is low, and most health indicators lagged those of wealthier economies even before the pandemic. According to the Bill & Melinda Gates Foundation, COVID-19 has reversed 2 decades of progress in vaccinating children against once-common childhood diseases worldwide. And since vaccine coverage is "a good proxy measure for how health systems are functioning," this may lead to serious and widespread regression in health metrics over time. In 2020, global vaccine coverage fell to levels last seen in the 1990s, or as the foundation put it: "...we've been set back about 25 years in 25 weeks."[4]

---

[4] Bill & Melinda Gates Foundation. 2020. COVID-19: A Global Perspective. *2020 Goalkeepers Report.* September. https://www. gatesfoundation.org/goalkeepers/report/2020-report/#GlobalPerspective.

Figure 5: Annual Per Capita Health Expenditure, Selected Economies in Developing Asia, 2016

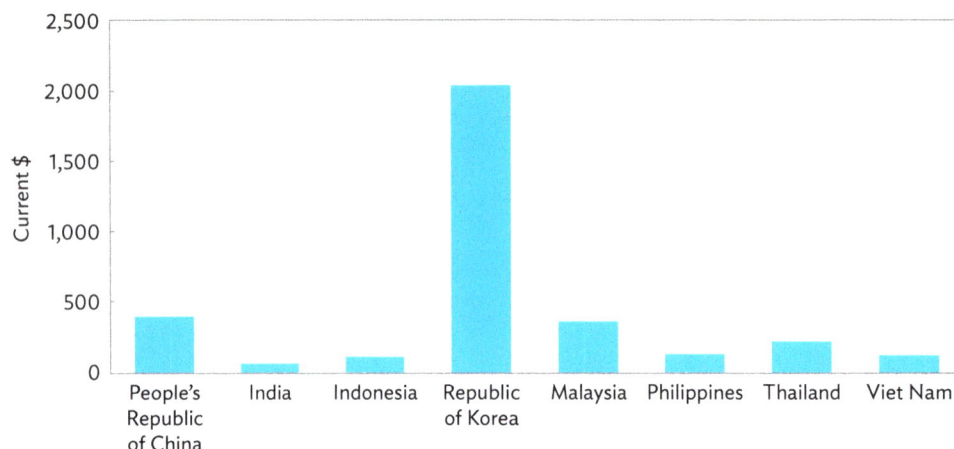

Source: Index Mundi. Current Health Expenditure Per Capita—Country Ranking. https://www.indexmundi.com/facts/indicators/SH.XPD.CHEX.PC.CD/rankings.

In the health-care sector over the long-term, social bonds may be used to finance

(i)   increased capacity and efficiency in providing health-care services and equipment (Box 2a),

(ii) medical research to prevent and alleviate future health-related disasters,

(iii) improvements in quality and provision of maternal health-care services,

(iv) improvements in the performance of public hospitals (Box 2b),

(v)   additional private sector health-care capacity focused on the mass market and not just those who can afford to pay large sums,

(vi) increased telehealth services including at-home care for the large numbers of people who do not have access to reliable medical care, and

(vii) a wider range of health-care services such as low-cost diagnostic and treatment devices to expand access.

Water and sanitation plays a role as well. One reason why COVID-19 and other diseases spread in developing economies is that billions of people lack adequate clean water for washing and sanitation. Frequent handwashing is one of the basic and effective ways for containing diseases generally, but underinvestment in water infrastructure has left many communities vulnerable. UN-Water calculates that $6.7 trillion in water infrastructure funding is needed by 2030—not just for sanitation needs to protect against communicable diseases but also "to tackle longer-term issues such as providing better irrigation to head off a potential food crisis."[5]

---

[5]   UN-Water. 2020. After the Pandemic We Must Build Hope Through Water and Sanitation. *UN-Water News.* 30 June. https://www.unwater.org/after-the-pandemic-building-hope-through-water-and-sanitation/.

Box 2a: Case Study—Nipro Corporation Social Bond for Securing Medical Supply Chains

In 2020, Nipro Corporation, a Japanese medical equipment and health-care supply manufacturing company, issued a JPY50 billion ($473 million equivalent) social bond focused on capital investment to secure medical supply chains, including vaccine-related supplies and dialysis treatments. As a "pure-play" health company that aims to "help solve the significant social issues of people's healthy lives," all of Nipro's current businesses are considered to be eligible for financing based on the company's Social Bond Framework. In particular, the company in its medium-term management plan aims to address social issues through investment in eligible projects, including ensuring a stable supply of medical devices and pharmaceutical materials, providing treatments to patients in remote areas, and enhancing the labor productivity of health-care professionals. Several of these focus areas dovetail with the Government of Japan's policy priorities regarding the need to secure access to medical supply chains for devices and active pharmaceutical ingredients, promoting the expansion of telemedicine, and fostering the domestic health-care profession in the face of an aging population.

The target projects corresponding to the International Capital Market Association's 2020 Social Bond Principles are access to basic services (health) with a target population of the "general public and particularly aging populations and people with disabilities, and underserved populations." The framework focuses on promoting health-related goals primarily linked to Sustainable Development Goal 3.

For impact reporting, the issuer commits to continuous disclosure of indicators, including domestic drug and medical device manufacturing capacity, dialysis patient capacity and number of training centers (outputs) against the number of drugs and devices sold, dialysis patients treated, and number of training center users (outcomes).

Source: Rating and Investment Information, Inc. Second Party Opinion: 2020. *Nipro Corporation Social Bond Framework*. https://www.r-i.co.jp/en/news_release_sof/2020/08/news_release_sof_20200807_eng.pdf.

Box 2b: Case Study—SFIL Group Social Bond for French Public Hospitals

SFIL, a French public development bank established for the country's public sector, issued two social bonds for a total of EUR2.0 billion ($2.2 billion equivalent) in 2019 and 2020, through its subsidiary, CAFFIL. The goal of the bonds is to provide financing for French public hospital systems. SFIL's Social Bond Framework applies to its health loan portfolio, which includes all public hospital loans issued by SFIL since its founding in 2013. This represents an organic extension of the issuer's mandate for financing national social infrastructure, and it can achieve considerable scale as approximately 60% of France's public sector investments are funded by policy banks like SFIL. The framework is designed to maximize social impact by determining eligibility for loans from the bond's proceeds based on SFIL's two-step credit analysis and an internal scoring methodology of all public hospital loans that assesses health-care added value along with creditworthiness.

The focus on public health and social infrastructure for SFIL's Social Bond Framework aligns it strongly with Sustainable Development Goal 3 (Good Health and Well-Being). For impact reporting, SFIL discloses transaction data such as the amount of proceeds allocated to its health loan portfolio, hospital capacity generated (in terms of spaces and beds), and number of hospital stays accommodated.

Source: Sustainalytics Second-Party Opinion. 2018. *SFIL Group Social Bond*. https://www.sustainalytics.com/wp-content/uploads/2018/10/SFIL-Group-Social-Bond-SPO.pdf.

Food Security
(SDG Linkages: SDG 1, 2, 3)

The Bill & Melinda Gates Foundation reports that people in both high- and low-income economies have reported skipping meals during the pandemic, creating "a nutritional catastrophe that will make the [pandemic] worse."[6] This is not a famine; food is widely available in most of the world, but it has become less accessible as low-income households reduce or redirect their spending.

COVID-19 has exposed vulnerabilities in global food systems by straining supplies, disrupting food chains, and increasing food insecurity for millions of people (Figure 6). According to the UN World Food Programme, hunger is increasing; the number of people confronting potentially life-threatening levels of food insecurity in the developing world is believed to have nearly doubled in 2020 to 265 million (Box 3).

Box 3: Case Study—African Development Bank "Fight COVID-19" Social Bond

In 2020, the African Development Bank (AfDB) issued a $3.1 billion "Fight COVID-19" social bond based on the bank's Social Bond Framework. AfDB's framework is built around the bank's mission to "spur sustainable economic development and social progress" in its regional member countries. In particular, the framework focuses on the bank's "High 5 Priority Areas for Transforming Africa", of which "Feed Africa" has an explicit focus on improving food security and nutrition on the continent. Eligible projects for bonds issued against the AfDB Social Bond Framework include agriculture-related developments such as agro-industrial processing zones; agricultural value chain development and enhancement; and support for farming skills, mechanization, and market development.

The "Feed Africa" component of the framework largely targets Sustainable Development Goal 2 (Zero Hunger). AfDB reports on the impacts of its green and social financing by disclosing the list of selected projects in an annual social bond newsletter, including disbursement levels and highlights of the key projects financed by the social bond portfolio.

Sources: Sustainalytics Second-Party Opinion. 2017. *African Development Bank Social Bond Framework*. https://www.icmagroup.org/Emails/icma-vcards/AfDB_SB_External%20Review%20Report.pdf; AfDB. 2020. *Green and Social Bond Newsletter—Issuer Number 6*. March. https://www.afdb.org/en/documents/green-and-social-bond-newsletter-issue-ndeg6-march-2020.

Based on Asian social bond issuance patterns, we estimate that allocations to health and food security remain at low levels on both an absolute basis and as a share of total issuance. This is possibly due to several factors. First, we calculate that only 24% of the social bond frameworks of Asian issuers reference health projects, compared to the non-Asia average of 38%. In comparison, the number of Asian social bond frameworks referencing SME financing is 47%, compared to the non-Asia average of 33%, potentially indicating different priorities between regions. Secondly, the COVID-19 pandemic has had relatively less impact in an epidemiological sense in the two main Asian issuers of social bonds, Japan and the Republic of Korea, compared to Europe and the US.

ICMA-compliant social bond issuance in Asian emerging economies in this issue area remains limited, indicating a potential gap for capital markets to fill with more social bonds targeted at developing Asia. We estimate that from 2017 to 2020, Asian social bond issuers raised only $1.54 billion equivalent through health-allocated issuance, with $1.12 billion equivalent, or over 70% of the total, raised by these issuers in 2020 alone (Figure 7). The majority of this issuance came from government foreign assistance agencies, health-care companies, and care-home operators in Japan, in addition to financial companies in the Republic of Korea (Figure 8).

---

[6] Footnote 4.

Figure 6: Prevalence of Food Insecurity by Asian Subregion in 2018

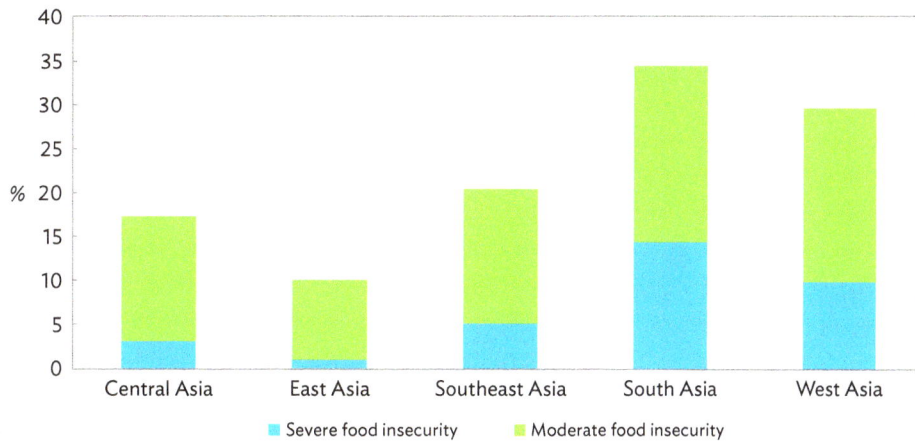

Note: The Food and Agriculture Organization of the United Nations defines food insecurity as the situation when people lack secure access to sufficient amounts of nutritious food for normal growth and development and an active and healthy life.

Source: Food and Agricultural Organization (FAO).

Figure 7: Amount of ICMA-Compliant Social Bond Issuance in Asia by SBP Project Type Allocation, 2017–2020 (USD-equivalent notional, estimated)

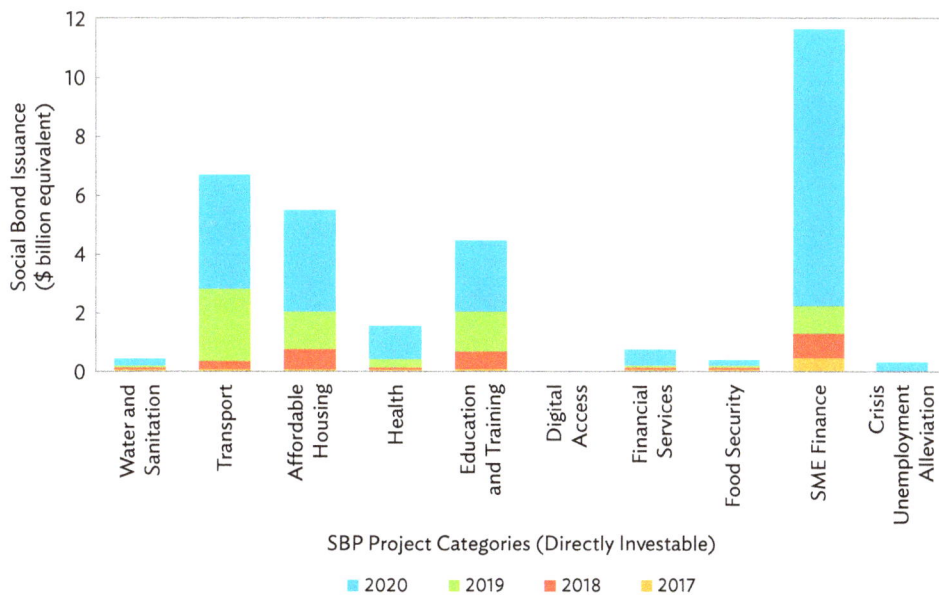

ICMA = International Capital Market Association, SBP = Social Bond Principles, SMEs = small and medium-sized enterprises, USD = United States dollar.

Sources: Authors' calculations based on review of Bloomberg data, issuer social bond frameworks, and reviewer second opinions.

Figure 8: Share of Issuer Social (and Sustainability) Bond Frameworks That Reference SBP Project Categories and Types, Issued from 2017 to 2020

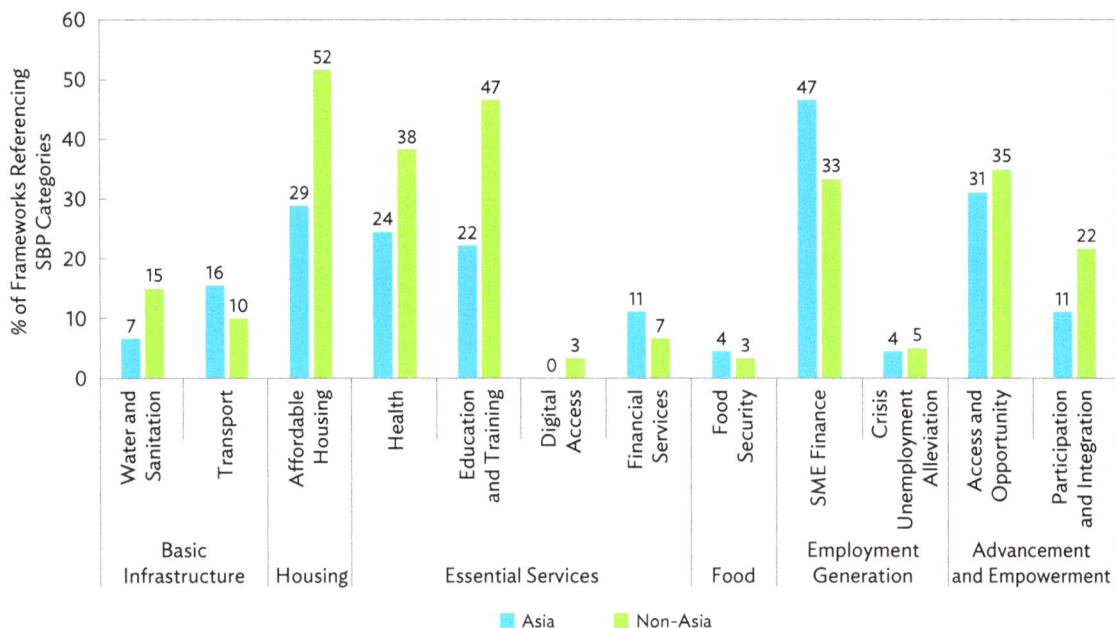

SBP = Social Bond Principles, SMEs = small and medium-sized enterprises.

Notes: Percentages are based on the count of framework text references, not the United States dollar equivalent notional amount. Totals do not sum to 100% due to overlapping designations.

Sources: Authors' calculations based on review of Bloomberg data, issuer social bond frameworks, and reviewer second opinions.

Small and Medium-Sized Enterprise Finance
(SDG Linkages: SDG 1, 5, 8, 9, 10)

Providing SME support to get businesses and people back on their feet again after the economic shock of the pandemic and associated lockdowns is a socioeconomic necessity with potentially large multiplier effects. SMEs account for more than 96% of all businesses in Asia and the Pacific, and more than two-thirds of the private sector workforce; they contribute 17% of gross domestic product (GDP) in some low-income economies such as India and 40%–50% of GDP in higher-income economies like Malaysia and Singapore (Figure 9).

Moreover, a few SMEs have the opportunity to make the leap from "garage to great." Just as Microsoft and Apple grew from start-ups to megacorporations, so did a few companies in developing Asia. Infosys, for example, started with capital of $250 and grew into a company with $12 billion in annual revenue and almost 250,000 employees in 2019. Other potentially great companies are currently in the start-up phase and can also prosper with the right level of financial support. Indeed, SMEs are often the lynchpins of their domestic economies, contributing to job creation, innovation, and productivity. Creating opportunities for SMEs in developing Asia "is an essential way to advance economic development and reduce poverty, and this will be even more critical during the recovery from the pandemic."[7]

---

[7] V. Erogbogbo and A. Khanna. 2020. SME Investing With a Gender Lens: The Key to COVID-19 Recovery in Emerging Markets. *Next Billion*. 20 August. https://nextbillion.net/sme-investing-gender-COVID-emerging-markets/.

Figure 9: Small and Medium-Sized Enterprise Employment Share in Selected Asian Economies

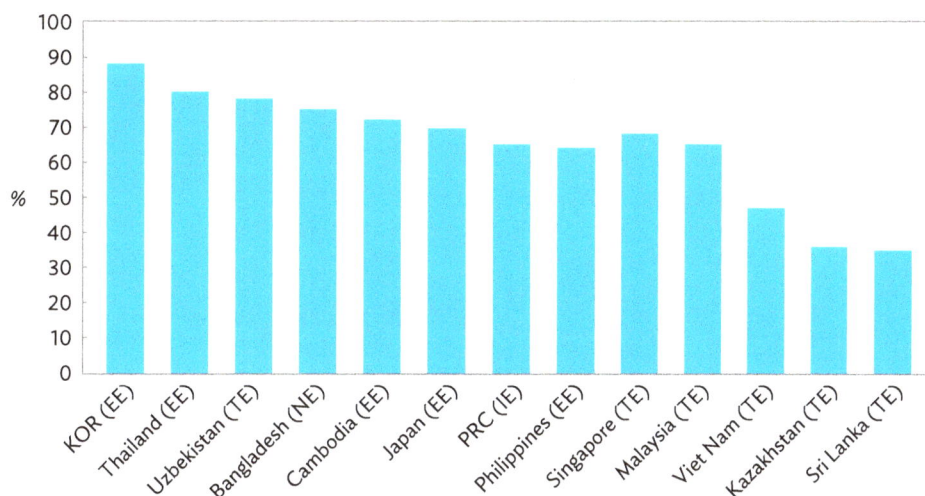

EE = enterprise employment, IE = industry employment, KOR = Republic of Korea, NE = nonagricultural employment, PRC = People's Republic of China, TE = total employment.

Note: Data are for the most recent year available in each economy during the period 2011–2016.

Source: Asian Development Bank Institute.

Even before the pandemic, SMEs faced a number of obstacles, most importantly the lack of access to finance. Without access to global capital markets or traditional bank financing, Asia's SME funding gap is likely to have increased since the pandemic began (Figure 10).

We find that SME finance is a leading issue for Asian social bonds, and issuance in this SBP project type increased tenfold from 2019 to 2020. Social bond issuance allocated to employment generation—including microfinance, SME finance, and socioeconomic crisis unemployment response—in Asia reached an estimated $9.84 billion equivalent in 2020, representing the single-largest SBP project category (Figure 11).

Figure 10: Small and Medium-Sized Enterprise Funding Gap in Selected Asian Economies, 2020

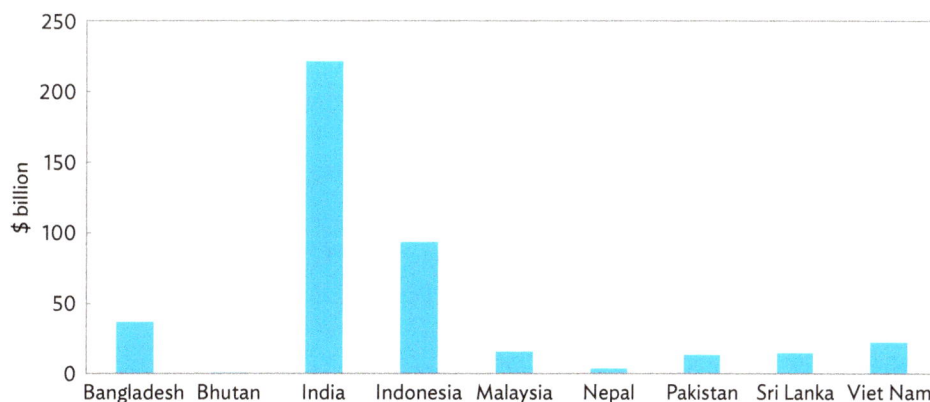

Source: SME Finance Forum. 2020. *MSME Finance Gap*. https://www.smefinanceforum.org/data-sites/msme-finance-gap.

Figure 11: Amount of ICMA-Compliant Social Bond Issuance in Asia by SBP Project Category Allocation, 2019 vs. 2020 (USD-equivalent notional, estimated)

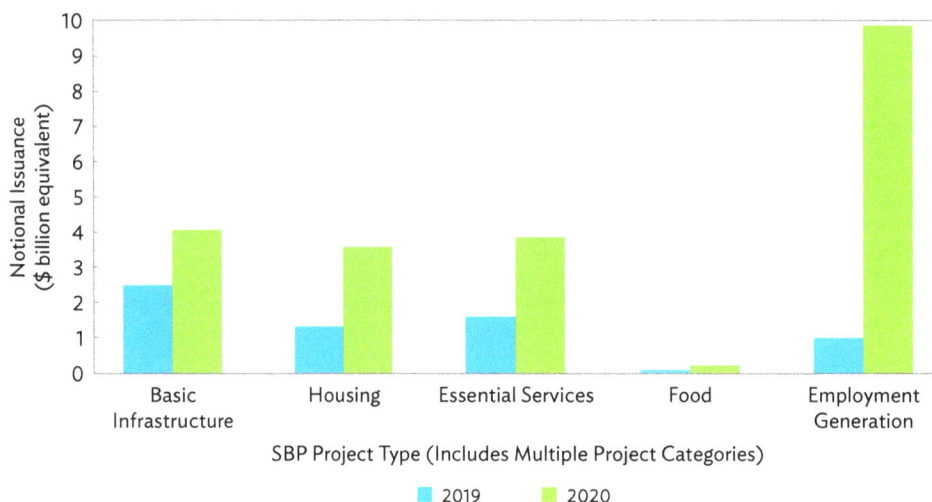

ICMA = International Capital Market Association, SBP = Social Bond Principles, USD= United States dollar.
Note: Zero social bond issuance by Asian issuers corresponding to the SBP Project Category "Socioeconomic Advancement and Empowerment" was recorded during the reference period, hence this group is not displayed.
Sources: Authors' calculations based on review of Bloomberg data, issuer social bond frameworks, and reviewer second opinions.

The amount of Asian social bond issuance that we estimate has been allocated to SME finance is, together with transport, one of only two project types where Asian social bond issuance exceeds the non-Asian total (Figure 12a).

Broken down by region and income level, we estimate that essentially all excluding high-income Asian social bond issuance in 2020 ($1.577 billion equivalent) was allocated to the SME finance project type, which is not surprising given the nature of the shock and economic structure of the region, and because all of the social bond issuers in this group happen to be financial corporations. This is a considerably different pattern compared with excluding high-income non-Asian social bond issuers, where we estimate that the majority of social bond project type allocations in 2020 went to affordable housing ($0.726 billion), with the balance going to health, education and training, and food security ($0.727 billion) (Figure 12b).

This focus on SME finance reflects recognition of the vulnerability of these enterprises to the pandemic's economic impact due to their limited financial resources and the tendency for SMEs to be concentrated in the services sector, where lockdowns and social distancing have had the greatest negative impact. On the other hand, targeted and concerted support for SMEs can be a highly effective way of helping people, communities, and countries in the region rebound from the pandemic. Financing opportunities in this area include the following examples:

(i)   credit facilities for SMEs to support employment generation (Box 4);
(ii) training programs for SME managers in cash management, budgeting, and bank and creditor relationships;
(iii) training programs for bankers to demonstrate the opportunity of lending to SMEs and to improve their ability to evaluate and manage financing for SMEs;
(iv) enabling financial inclusion for women; and
(v)   training for displaced workers to help them adapt to different industries.

Figure 12a: Asian and Non-Asian ICMA-Compliant Social Bond Issuance by SBP Project Type, 2020 (USD-equivalent notional, estimated)

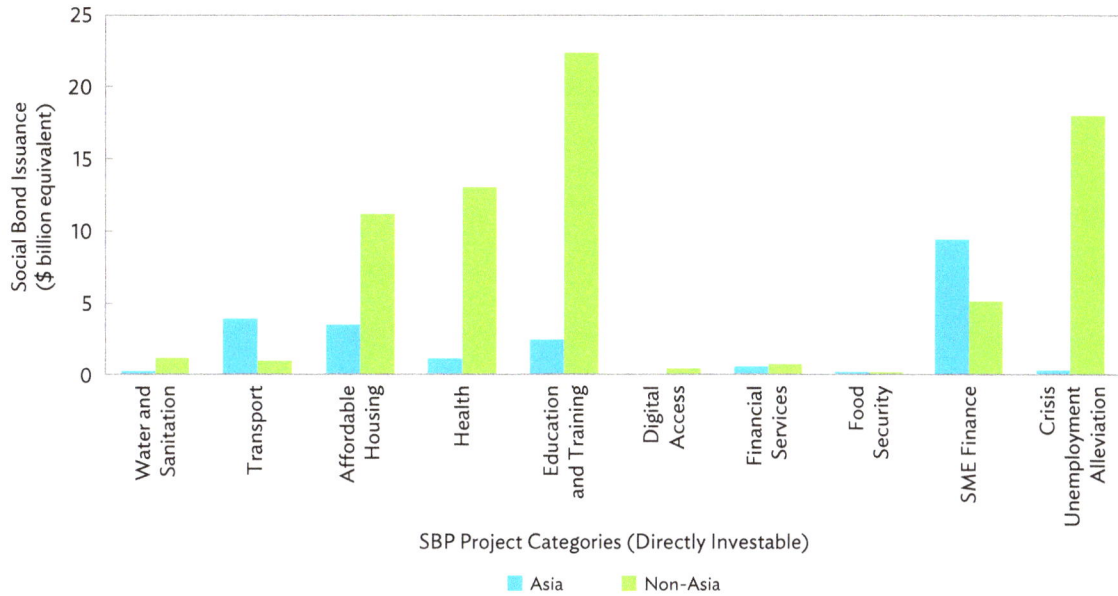

ICMA = International Capital Market Association, SBP = Social Bond Principles, SMEs = small and medium-sized enterprises, USD = United States dollar.

Sources: Authors' calculations based on review of Bloomberg data, issuer social bond frameworks, and reviewer second opinions.

Figure 12b: Excluding High-Income Asian and Non-Asian ICMA-Compliant Social Bond Issuance by SBP Project Type, 2020 (USD-equivalent notional, estimated)

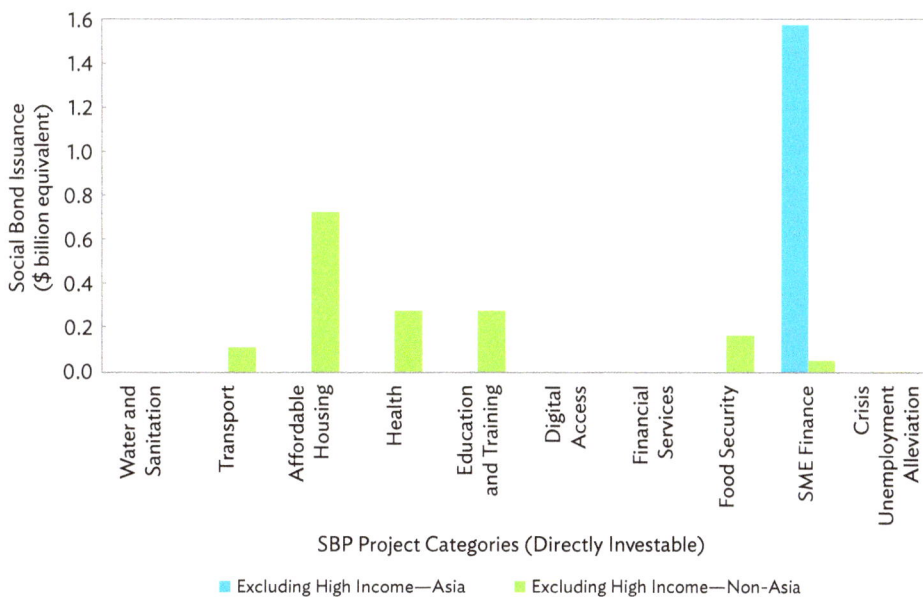

ICMA = International Capital Market Association, SBP = Social Bond Principles, SMEs = small and medium-sized enterprises, USD = United States dollar.

Sources: Authors' calculations based on review of Bloomberg data, issuer social bond frameworks, and reviewer second opinions.

Box 4: Case Study—Bank of the Philippine Islands COVID-19 Action Response Bonds for MSME Financing

In August 2020, the Bank of the Philippine Islands issued a PHP21.5 billion ($438 million equivalent) social bond to finance or refinance loans to micro, small, and medium-sized enterprises (MSMEs). The bank described its targeted impact as a response to coronavirus disease (COVID-19) through lending support to MSMEs negatively affected by both natural and health disasters. The bank's Sustainable Funding Framework is intended to support the ability of MSMEs to respond to disruptions in order to minimize economic and social impacts. This aligns with the Government of the Philippines' MSME Development Plan, 2017–2022, which is a policy strategy that seeks to make local businesses more resilient to natural hazards.

The target population is twofold. It directly reaches MSMEs that have been significantly affected by the pandemic; and indirectly, it reaches employees of MSMEs, which account for 60% of the Philippines' total labor force. There are three Sustainable Development Goal (SDG) linkages: SDG 8 (Decent Work and Economic Growth); SDG 9 (Industry, Innovation, and Infrastructure); and SDG 10 (Reduced Inequalities). The bank will report on the social bond's impact by tracking the number of loans made to MSMEs and the total monetary value of these loans with a dedicated register, and by disclosing the details annually as part of the bank's annual integrated report. The second-party opinion by Sustainalytics encouraged the bank to disclose the MSMEs that had been financed and provide details on the level of impact achieved through the social lending program.

Notably, this social bond is compliant with the Association of Southeast Asian Nations Social Bond Standards.

Source: Sustainalytics Second-Party Opinion. 2020. *Bank of the Philippine Islands Sustainable Funding Framework*. https://www.bpiexpressonline.com/media/uploads/5ee07272d52ba_SPO_-_BPI_Sustainable_Funding_Framework.pdf.

Education and Training
(SDG Linkages: SDG 1, 4, 5, 8, 9, 10)

The pandemic has negatively impacted educational opportunities in developing economies, dramatically widening the educational deficit. The Education Commission reports: "The world is in the midst of an unprecedented global crisis as a result of COVID-19 that will be felt for generations." Even prior to the crisis, the Education Commission expressed concern that 250 million children worldwide were out of school and more than 550 million were in school but unable to learn basic skills.[8]

The poorest and most marginalized children—including girls, refugees, and those living in extreme poverty—are at the greatest risk. This threatens future generations by preventing children from realizing their potential to contribute to socioeconomic development in their home countries and communities.

Funders need not only to build schools and hire teachers but also to demand that this money delivers real impact. Schools must be able to demonstrate clear outcomes in terms of improved learning levels and readiness skills. In this area, a focus on outcome measurement is especially critical. Good education is not just a matter of counting heads—for example, tallying the number of children who attend school—but of measuring impact. How many learners achieved improved scores on standardized tests? How many achieved financial literacy? Are low-income students achieving at the same levels as higher-income children? To ensure impact, capital providers should demand rigorous management and measurement of performance metrics.

Box 5 discusses a social bond in France that supports job training programs.

---

[8]   The Education Commission. *Finance Transformation: Mobilizing More and Better Education Investments*. https://educationcommission.org/international-finance-facility-education/ (accessed 20 October 2020).

Box 5: Case Study—Unédic Social Bond Program

In 2020, Unédic, a French unemployment insurance management body, issued a series of five social bonds totaling EUR17 billion ($19.3 billion equivalent) through the agency's social bond framework. Unédic's framework is intended to promote the government agency's mission of supporting sustainable employment by both providing unemployment insurance in France (the "protection" mission) and assisting workers' professional reintegration through education (retraining) and professional skills and qualifications development (the "support" mission). Developed and published in May 2020, the agency's framework is aimed at addressing unemployment and the resulting socioeconomic reintegration challenges facing France as a result of the coronavirus disease (COVID-19) pandemic, and thus support the country's socioeconomic priorities directly. Although the bulk of financing is likely to be directed to unemployment benefit payments for socioeconomic needs, the addition of training and reskilling programs to the framework presents an innovative and more sustainable policy approach by tying in education and (re)training to the pandemic response.

The target project areas corresponding to the International Capital Market Association's 2020 Social Bond Principles are socioeconomic development and access to basic services (education and professional training) with a target population of unemployed individuals living under the poverty line and individuals with little education or no diploma. The social issues relevant to the theme of education and training targeted by the framework include programs aimed at helping the return to work and professional (re)integration, skills and qualifications development, and re-employment and training. The framework promotes training-related goals in the areas of education, work, and inequality through linkages to Sustainable Development Goal (SDG) 1 (No Poverty), SDG 4 (Quality Education), SDG 8 (Decent Work and Economic Growth), and SDG 10 (Reduced Inequalities).

The issuer commits to report an indicative list of social impact indicators including the amount of funds allocated, the breakdown of funds assigned by eligible category and underlying program, and Unédic's share when cofinancing programs with other entities. Impact data and reporting are to be submitted to the Social Bond Committee for review, audited by an external auditor, and published on Unédic's website on an annual basis. However, the framework acknowledges that while data on the situation of jobseekers can be provided for perspective, no direct causal link can be made between the social bond financing and macro-social indicators due to the systematic nature of unemployment insurance programs. To overcome these data challenges, the issuer proposes to disclose in-depth investigations (e.g., longitudinal monitoring, efficacy analysis using control groups, interviews, and satisfaction surveys) that measure the efficiency and indirect impacts of the programs provided.

Sources: ISS ESG Second-Party Opinion. 2020. *Unédic. Sustainability Quality of the Issuer and Social Bond Programme.* https://www.icmagroup.org/assets/Uploads/Unedic_External-Review-Report.pdf; Unédic. Social Bond Framework. 2020. https://www.unedic.org/sites/default/files/2020-05/Social%20Bond%20Framework%20Un%C3%A9dic_Final%20 Version_ENG.pdf [in English].

Girls' Education
(SDG Linkages: SDG 1, 4, 5, 10)

Girls' education is not only a basic human right; it is also one of the most effective ways to drive sustainable development, improve health, reduce conflict, and save lives (Box 6). But according to The Asia Foundation, even before the pandemic, "growing inequality in a number of Asian countries [was] profoundly affecting girls' access to education… " (Table 3). This limits women's participation in science, technology, engineering, and mathematics-related fields, thus limiting the scope of job opportunities for them; it also increases the incidence of child marriage for young girls.[9]

---

[9] J. Sloan. 2019. It's Time for Large-Scale Investment in Girls' Education Across Asia. *The Asia Foundation.* 20 November. https://reliefweb.int/ report/world/it-s-time-large-scale-investment-girls-education-across-asia.

Table 3: Gender Gap Index Overall and in Educational Attainment by Subregion, Pre-Pandemic 2020

	Eastern Europe and Central Asia	East Asia and the Pacific	South Asia
Overall Index Score	0.715	0.685	0.661
Educational Attainment	0.998	0.976	0.943

Note: The Global Gender Gap index quantifies the gaps between men and women in four key areas: economic participation and opportunity, educational attainment, health and survival, and political empowerment.
Source: World Economic Forum. 2020. Global Gender Gap Index. http://www3.weforum.org/docs/WEF_GGGR_2020.pdf.

At the height of the pandemic lockdowns, schools were closed in 192 economies, affecting 1.6 billion students. The United Nations Educational, Scientific and Cultural Organization (UNESCO) reports that 11 million girls are now at risk of never returning to school, potentially increasing the gender gap in educational attainment. The 2014 Ebola outbreak in West Africa provides evidence; poor families needed their children to earn money during the crisis, and children who found work were rarely encouraged to return to school when it reopened.[10] When the schools did reopen, girls were less likely to return than boys, thus closing off opportunities for themselves and their future families.

If this trend is not reversed, it could have repercussions for many years to come. An education adviser at UNICEF East Asia and Pacific warns that, with regard to girls' education, the region "will be going backward several years." The United Nations Children's Fund (UNICEF) adviser further stated: "We'll lose progress. The spillover effect will be massive because it may also impact the generation after this one. It can take us so many years to get back to where we were before. This won't help the Asian economy."[11]

Gender Equity
(SDG Linkages: SDG 1, 5, 8, 10)

Girls' education is a subset of the globally important issue of gender equity. The pandemic has led to gender-differentiated impacts in Asia and the Pacific, and this requires gender-differentiated responses. COVID-19 susceptibility and mortality is greater among men, yet the socioeconomic impact of the pandemic falls more heavily on women. Unpaid care work—such as cooking, cleaning, and caring for children and sick relatives—is typically provided by women. With children at home instead of in school, men at home instead of at work, and many sick people at home instead of in hospitals, this unpaid care work has relatively increased—so the distribution of such labor is becoming more lopsided, not less.[12] Gender inequality in the region was relatively high pre-pandemic, and it has been worsened by the COVID-19 shock.

Social bonds can help reduce gender inequity and empower women; this is good for both business and for society. Corporates can raise funds through social bonds to increase women's participation in their local economies, improve working conditions for female employees, decrease the digital divide between men and women, and provide capital for underfunded women-owned SMEs (Box 7).

---

[10] S. Giannini. 2020. COVID-19 school closures around the world will hit girls hardest. UNESCO. https://en.unesco.org/news/covid-19-school-closures-around-world-will-hit-girls-hardest.

[11] R. Thanthong-Knight. 2020. Girls Are Quitting School To Work in Virus-Battered Asia. *Bloomberg*. 19 September. https://www.bloomberg.com/news/articles/2020-09-19/girls-are-quitting-school-to-work-in-virus-battered-rural-asia.

[12] Footnote 4.

Box 6: Case Study—Educate Girls Development Impact Bond in Rajasthan, India

This project was funded by India's first development impact bond (DIB) and was led by Educate Girls, a nongovernment organization working to increase the enrollment of girls in public schools in Rajasthan, India, and to improve their learning outcomes. In rural areas of Rajasthan, which are dominated by subsistence agriculture, about 10% of girls aged 11–14 years do not attend school, mainly because they are needed to add to family income or care for siblings. The quality of girls' education in these areas is also a concern, as the female literacy rate in 2011 was just 52%, compared to 79% for men and the national average of 65% for women.

When the 3-year project concluded, the outside evaluator found that there was reason to celebrate: the project exceeded the pre-agreed performance metrics on both enrollment and learning outcomes, giving investors a modest financial return and enabling Educate Girls to substantially scale up its funding and impact. The pay-for-success-based DIB structure enabled project leaders to adjust their methods in real time and improve efficiency through active performance management.

Despite its good intentions, however, it is hard to hold up the Educate Girls DIB as a funding structure worthy of emulation. Development of the project began in 2013, but complex negotiations and calculations with the various players meant that the program did not actually launch until 2015; remarkably, the direct project budget of $270,000 was less than the evaluation cost of $300,000. Total costs, including management expenses and funds to publicly communicate the results, were estimated at about $1 million.

Further, the DIB did not bring new, or private, capital to the project. It merely passed money from one philanthropy to another; the up-front investor was UBS Optimus Foundation, which was repaid by the outcome payor, the Children's Investment Fund Foundation. Also, the evaluation results prove only that the Educate Girls intervention method was a success, not that the DIB financing mechanism added value to the project. In fact, the complexity and long lead time demanded by this process suggest that its benefits did not exceed its costs.

The value of the project, however, is still significant. It underlined the need for quality girls' education in poor, rural areas of Asia, it introduced better teacher training and management to manage education quality, and it included a real-time assessment to enable real-time performance improvement. This creates an opportunity to scale up this type of project using private capital such as social bonds throughout the region.

Sources: A. Saldinger. 2018. The Educate Girls DIB Exceeded Its Goals: How Did They Do It and What Does It Mean? *Devex*. 13 July. https://www.devex.com/news/the-educate-girls-dib-exceeded-its-goals-how-did-they-do-it-and-what-does-it-mean-93112; I. Boggild-Jones and E. Gustafsson-Wright. 2018. World's First Development Impact Bond for Education Shows Successful Achievement of Outcomes in Its Final Year. *Brookings*. 13 July. https://www.brookings.edu/blog/education-plus-development/2018/07/13/worlds-first-development-impact-bond-for-education-shows-successful-achievement-of-outcomes-in-its-final-year/.

Box 7: Case Study—Bank of Ayudhya (Krungsri) Social Bond for Women's Small and Medium-Sized Enterprise Finance

In October 2019, the Bank of Ayudhya (Krungsri) issued a social bond in Thailand to finance the growth of women-led small and medium-sized enterprises (SMEs). The bond raised $220 million and was, notably, the first bank-issued gender bond in Asia and the Pacific. It was also the first social bond issuance in developing Asia that was in compliance with both the International Capital Market Association Social Bond Principles and the Association of Southeast Asian Nations Social Bond Standards.

The impact areas addressed by this bond are gender equity; women-led SME support; financial inclusion for the underserved; the promotion of sustainable, resilient, and inclusive growth; and the support of women as the drivers of the Thai economy and society. The bond was aligned with Sustainable Development Goal (SDG) 5, SDG 8, SDG 9, SDG 10, and SDG 17.

The bond's impact will be tracked by following employment generation through women-owned SMEs, socioeconomic advancement through financing to low-income women and disadvantaged female groups, and total SME loans outstanding and use of proceeds.

Source: Bank of Ayudhya (Krungsri).

We find that of the social bond frameworks in our global database, only 15% reference SDG 5 (Gender Equality). On the other hand, of the social bond frameworks that specify a target population based on demographic groupings (e.g., women, minorities, the elderly, young people, and young families), 23% of the social bond frameworks of Asian issuers include women within the target population(s), compared to only 10% of social bond frameworks among non-Asian issuers. Taking action to advance gender equality could add $13 trillion to global GDP by 2030 compared to a gender-regressive scenario, according to McKinsey & Company.[13]

Resilience to Disasters
(SDG Linkages: SDG 1, 2, 3, 6, 8, 11, 13)

The global response to the COVID-19 pandemic emphasizes building resilience to future shocks like natural disasters. Thus, there is an opportunity now to harness investor interest and attention to invest in resilience by addressing these needs.[14] Social bonds can be used to fund projects that reduce the downside impact of future crises and spur resilience and recovery for when disasters do strike (Box 8).

Box 8: Case Study—NEXCO East Social Bonds

Between 2019 and 2020, East Nippon Express Co., Ltd (NEXCO East), the Japanese expressway operator, issued a series of 18 social bonds amounting to JPY620 billion ($5.8 billion equivalent) through the company's social finance framework. NEXCO East's framework is meant to finance transport infrastructure construction and resiliency, including projects for reinforcing seismic resistance and expanding capacity along evacuation routes. In this way, the issuer's framework provides direct and indirect support to two Government of Japan national policies—the Basic Plan for Extending Service Life of Infrastructure and the Basic Plan for National Resilience—by responding to social issues based on the national land plan and other priorities.

The target projects correspond to the International Capital Market Association's 2020 Social Bond Principle of affordable basic infrastructure, with a target population of the general public during normal times and with an explicit focus on vulnerable groups, including as a result of national disasters, during emergencies. The social issues relevant to the theme of resiliency targeted by the framework include reduction of risks from earthquakes and tsunamis, and intensifying weather hazards, as well as measures to address aging infrastructure. The framework promotes resiliency-related goals covering issues of safety, infrastructure, climate-change countermeasures, and sustainable communities through linkages to Sustainable Development Goal (SDG) 3, SDG 8, SDG 9, SDG 11, and SDG 13.

The issuer will report on the social impacts primarily by disclosing its funding allocation and project status for reconstruction, maintenance and repair projects, as well as disaster-prevention and safety measurements as part of the issuer's existing corporate social responsibility reporting. The second-party opinion by Rating & Investment Information, Inc. highlighted the issuer's comprehensive approach to assessing the positive and negative impacts at the direct and indirect level, in both local and wide-areas, based on a comparison of social outcomes and the feasibility of negative impact mitigation measures.

Source: R&I Second Opinions. 2020. *East Nippon Expressway Co., Ltd. Social Finance Framework*. https://www.r-i.co.jp/en/news_release_sof/2020/06/news_release_sof_20200610_01_eng.pdf.

---

[13] A. Madgavkar, O. White, M. Krishnan, D. Mahajan, and X. Azcue. 2020. *COVID-19 and Gender Equality: Countering the Regressive Effects. McKinsey Global Institute.* https://www.mckinsey.com/featured-insights/future-of-work/COVID-19-and-gender-equality-countering-the-regressive-effects.

[14] H. Lee. 2020. COVID's Spreading Fast Because Billions Don't Have Water to Wash. *Bloomberg.* 7 August. https://www.bloomberg.com/news/articles/2020-08-07/COVID-s-spreading-fast-because-billions-don-t-have-water-to-wash.

Digital Access and Financial Services
(SDG Linkages: SDG 3, 4, 5, 8, 9, 10, 11)

Another area of inequality highlighted by the pandemic is infrastructure, particularly digital infrastructure and the digital divide. While physical infrastructure is obviously required for clean water, health-care facilities, and transport—the need for equal and reliable access to information technology has been revealed as particularly pressing. Those without access to the internet and communications lack access to public health information and educational opportunities; they also risk being left behind in an increasingly digital economy.[15]

Digital infrastructure is necessary not only to better connect students with educators but also to deliver high-quality and cost-efficient education. Access to technology is also important for financial inclusion, especially for women. Digitization of business processes extends beyond the finance sector; SMEs, tourist-related businesses, education, and health care increasingly require access to technology for connecting to customers and delivering goods and services throughout the economy (Box 9).

Box 9: Case Study—Credit Agricole SA Social Bonds

In late 2020, Credit Agricole SA, a French banking group, issued a EUR1 billion ($1.2 billion equivalent) bond through the company's social bond framework. Credit Agricole SA's framework is meant to support social and economic development via bank financing to a wide range of sectors including (but not limited to) regional economic development through information and communications technology access in rural areas, and access to finance for micro, small, and medium-sized enterprises (MSMEs) specifically targeted to socioeconomically disadvantaged areas in the issuer's home country of France. By targeting certain aspects of inequality related to regional disparities, the issuer's framework is positioned to contribute to important social challenges while boosting national growth and (potentially) the issuer's own financial performance over time.

The relevant target projects corresponding to the International Capital Market Association's 2020 Social Bond Principles are small and medium-sized enterprise (SME) financing and information and communication technology access, with specific targeting of populations in socioeconomically disadvantaged areas in France and the general public and unserved populations in rural areas. Falling under the heading of territorial economic development, these projects aim to generate faster economic growth through more employment and reduced inequalities. The framework promotes a wide variety of financing areas of which digital and financial inclusion are an important part, with linkages to Sustainable Development Goal (SDG) 8, SDG 9, SDG 10, and SDG 11, among others.

The issuer commits to provide impact reporting based on the social bond's allocation of proceeds among project categories, expected social benefits of the eligible categories, and material developments, including environmental, social, and governance controversies related to project financing. Specific to digital and financial access projects, the issuer will report on the following outputs and outcomes: number of SME loans provided, number of people employed by financed SMEs, and number of loans granted to information and communication technology infrastructure and rural development projects. The issuer will also provide estimates of social impact measures such as the absolute and relative increase in people attaining digital connectivity. The issuer's corporate structure as a network of regional and local banking cooperatives gives the bank a potentially unique position to effectively provide financing to alleviate regional socioeconomic disparities in France.

Source: Vigeo-Eiris Second-Party Opinion. 2020. *Crédit Agricole SA Social Bond Framework*. https://vigeo-eiris.com/wp-content/uploads/2020/12/20201126_ve_spo_credit-agricole_vf.pdf.

---

[15] United Nations Development Programme Bureau for Asia and the Pacific. 2020. *The Social and Economic Impact of COVID-19 in the Asia-Pacific Region*. https://www.undp.org/publications/social-and-economic-impact-covid-19-asia-pacific-region.

At present, women in low- and middle-income economies are less likely than men to use financial services (a gap of 9 percentage points) or own mobile phones (8 percentage points) (GSMA 2020).[16] Yet, mobile money services may actually close the gender gap in financial inclusion more quickly than traditional banking products. The ability to make and receive digital payments provides a path forward in financial inclusion for women, which is a step toward gender equity and women's empowerment in the developing world.

For SMEs, digitization "strengthens productivity and improves their access to finance markets." One survey found that 49% of SME chief executive officers believe that technology "levels the playing field for small businesses versus larger corporations." And at the macro level, the digitization of SMEs can "also enhance a country's economic activity." It is estimated that the digitization of SMEs among member countries of the Association of Southeast Asian Nations could add $1.1 trillion to regional GDP by 2025.[17]

Broadband access for underserved populations has been one of the use-of-proceeds areas for social bonds since the SBP launch in 2017, but COVID-19 has highlighted its urgency. As of 2020, only four social bond frameworks by issuers of publicly tendered social bonds, including the Asian Development Bank, specifically referenced the digital access ICMA project type, making it the rarest target for social bond projects. Attention given to this issue is likely to grow as the prevalence of virtual education and commerce is likely to become permanent, thus offering a new angle for applying the SBP to assist in recovery.

Poverty and Inequality
(SDG Linkages: SDG 1, 4, 5, 8, 10)

The poor are the hardest hit by the health, social, and economic crisis spawned by COVID-19. The pandemic has caused job and income losses in Asia and the Pacific, with a disproportionately large impact on informal employment, as noted above. It has particularly impacted industries employing many people just above the poverty line, such as in tourism, textile manufacturing, and low-skilled service sectors.

Daily and hourly laborers, domestic and cross-border migrants alike, have lost jobs and income overnight; and these groups are most likely to have limited or no access to social safety nets or cash savings. Of the total workforce in Asia and the Pacific, which was estimated at 1.9 billion in 2019, around two-thirds (1.3 billion) are informally employed and at greatest risk according to the UN.[18]

While poverty has declined substantially in Asia and the Pacific over the past several decades, its rate of reduction has slowed since 2010, and the pandemic is certain to reverse a number of those gains. The Bill & Melinda Gates Foundation estimated that COVID-19 had driven nearly 37 million people into extreme poverty worldwide as of September 2020; others estimate that it could push 100 million back below the poverty line.[19] Inequality is also expected to increase in countries with weak social and labor protections. This makes achievement of the SDGs by 2030 a near impossibility in such countries (Box 10).

---

[16] GSMA. 2020. Connected Women: The Mobile Gender Gap Report 2020. https://www.gsma.com/mobilefordevelopment/wp-content/uploads/2020/05/GSMA-The-Mobile-Gender-Gap-Report-2020.pdf.

[17] M. Miller, L. Klapper, G. Teima, and M. Gamser. 2020. How Can Digital Financial Services Help a World Coping with COVID-19? *World Bank Blogs.* 3 August. https://blogs.worldbank.org/psd/how-can-digital-financial-services-help-world-coping-COVID-19.

[18] United Nations Development Programme Bureau for Asia and the Pacific. 2020. *The Social and Economic Impact of COVID-19 in the Asia-Pacific Region.* https://www.undp.org/content/undp/en/home/librarypage/crisis-prevention-and-recovery/the-social-and-economic-impact-of-covid-19-in-asia-pacific.html.

[19] Footnote 4.

Box 10: Case Study—Region Wallonne Belgium Social Bond

In the middle of 2020, Region Wallonne Belgium, one of the three regional authorities comprising the federal state of Belgium, issued a EUR1 billion ($1.2 billion equivalent) social and coronavirus disease (COVID-19) response bond. The proceeds of this issue were intended to finance exceptional, one-time fixed compensation measures to mitigate the socioeconomic crisis and to provide funding to support regional health care and social structures and services. This social bond was issued under the region's existing Sustainability Bond Framework and based on the pool of eligible expenditures related to socioeconomic advancement and empowerment, and access to basic services and public infrastructure, in line with the region's five identified challenges, particularly "Live Together and Fight Against Poverty."

The relevant target projects corresponding to the International Capital Market Association's 2020 Social Bond Principles are access and opportunity, and participation and integration, with the specific targeting of citizens in the Walloon Region who are low-income, indebted, elderly, homeless, or disabled. As a regional government issuer, the use of proceeds for dedicated programs related to local development, poverty alleviation, support for disabled and elderly citizens, and health-care facilities can be directly tied to government policies and priority areas in society. For the COVID-19 response bond specifically, the project categories are linked to Sustainable Development Goal (SDG) 1, SDG 3, and SDG 10.

Based on the region's overarching Sustainability Bond Framework, impact reporting is based on the social bond's allocation of proceeds at the eligible category levels, including a brief list and description of certain eligible projects per financed category, and relevant social benefits, output, and impact indicators—all subject to data availability. For the COVID-19 response bond specifically, the issuer will add reporting indicators related to COVID-19 related use of proceeds such as the number of health care and social structures and services supported, and R&D expenditures against COVID-19. The original second-party opinion by Vigeo-Eiris suggested the issuer commit to add further indicators at the project level after issuance has taken place and funding disbursement has been decided, as well as reporting on material developments relating to the underlying projects such as environmental, social, and governance controversies or project modifications.

Sources: Vigeo-Eiris Second-Party Opinion. 2020. *Walloon Region's Sustainable Bond Framework*. https://www.wallonie. be/sites/default/files/2020-03/20200330_vigeo_eiris_spo_walloon_region_vf.pdf; Region Wallonne. 2020. *Investor Presentation*. https://www.wallonie.be/sites/default/files/2020-05/wallonia_sb2020_investor_presentation_h1_2020. pdf.

Social Impact Measurement—Supporting a Well-Functioning Social Bond Market

3

The unresolved question of social impact measurement is key to rebuilding. Social and all other environmental, social, and governance (ESG)-linked bonds are only as good as the impact they achieve, so it is imperative that they are assessed according to as rigorous impact measurement as is practicable. Indeed, as the ESG bond market expanded sharply in 2020, "social washing," in which issuers claim that the funds will be used for worthy areas but the money ends up elsewhere, was a significant concern.[20] Indeed, you cannot manage what you do not measure.

But practicability is a constraint, and the question of social impact measurement is by no means a settled issue. The field is undergoing much experimentation and innovation that is largely useful and instructive, but it is important to note that there is no widespread agreement on a single model of assessment. Debate and dissension is appropriate, however, as the market explores how best to undertake social impact measurement, which itself is to some degree an attempt to quantify the unquantifiable.

According to a forthcoming working paper from the Asian Development Bank, impact is defined as "a positive change made in alignment with organization objectives that is additional and can be measured." While environmental impact is generally physical in nature and relatively easier to measure, improvements in social welfare are difficult to standardize and assess, as levels of analysis and perspectives vary. The working paper argues that effective measurement and management is essential to the effective allocation of sustainable finance. While many competing models exist, there is not yet a set of agreed standards—but there are also opportunities thanks to new regulatory policies on social and environmental disclosure beyond ESG, as well as "new impact data capture technologies."[21]

A few principles should be applied to social impact measurement:

(i) There should be strict adherence to the principle of additionality; that is, that the social project should provide additional benefits to the population being served, which would not have accrued in the absence of the project.

(ii) Impact measurement should be as consistent, objective, and verifiable as possible. This does not rule out surveys, which are essentially subjective, but it does suggest that they should be supported by other methodologies.

(iii) It is desirable to distinguish correlation from causality where possible. This suggests that randomized controlled trials are the gold standard; but they are very expensive and can lead to the ethical dilemma of depriving a population of needed services in order to secure a control group.[22]

---

[20] C. Hodgson. 2020. COVID-19 Bonds Drive "Sustainable" Debt as Green Issuance Fades. *Financial Times*. 17 August. https://www.ft.com/content/6102f537-dec1-4406-847d-b8d5ab4f5dad.

[21] A. Nicholls. 2021. *Using Social Bonds to Achieve Meaningful Impact in Developing Asia*. Asian Development Bank.

[22] Randomized controlled trials are used to reduce certain types of bias by randomly allocating subjects to two or more groups, treating them differently, and comparing the results. A project may assign half of its participants to receive an intervention being assessed, for example, while the other participants (the control group) does not receive the intervention.

(iv)   Social impact measurement techniques should determine real impact beyond just "counting heads" as data for the sake of data.

(v)   Social impact measurement should be comparable across projects within the same and different project categories to the extent possible. Social projects do not lend themselves to comparability as readily as environmental projects, as social outcomes frequently vary from project to project.

When it comes to measuring social impact, these principles are often more aspirational than practical. There is an inherent contradiction in quantifying social impact; precision says nothing about accuracy. Impact metrics in the green bond market are generally more standardized, where there are physical parameters to measure, but not yet in the social bond market. One lesson from the green bond market is that markets favor scalability and comparability; impractical and overly elaborate social metrics may be of limited value to the market.

Transparency in use of proceeds and impact measurement is easier said than done. A counting heads or output-based approach does not measure impact well; it may just measure the number of people served regardless of quality or outcomes. A financial inclusion training program may consider itself successful because it has served a large number of women; however, this does not measure the impact of the program on the women's lives. It is better to ask, for example: How many women opened and maintained bank accounts after the program or took out loans? How many experienced an improvement in their economic position or were able to educate their children? While counting heads can serve as a rough guide to investors seeking social impact data, it is incomplete at best and an invitation to social washing at worst.

While prioritizing outcomes rather than outputs for measurement is ideal in theory, outcomes may take years to materialize (as with early childhood education)—if at all. Moreover, success may be difficult to measure, and it is difficult to distinguish correlation from causality.

Social impact measurement, in which "contexts, missions, definitions, measurement approaches, and values differ," is especially challenging. This "comparison problem" not only affects good decision-making, but also the ability to report on impact at the investment portfolio level.[23] As a result, many impact investors "are instead choosing to create specifically tailored measurement tools, such as impact scorecards or investor-specific impact frameworks, in lieu of using a more standardized measurement tool, external taxonomies, or standards."[24]

In the face of these challenges, some organizations are working to develop frameworks for social impact investment measurement. Some frameworks may be of limited direct value for mainstream bond investors but could be valuable as a reference in this emerging area.

---

[23] K. Ruff and S. Olsen. 2016. The Next Frontier in Social Impact Measurement Isn't Measurement At All. *Stanford Social Innovation Review*. 10 May. https://ssir.org/articles/entry/next_frontier_in_social_impact_measurement#.

[24] L. Aquino-Hagedorn and S. Doran. 2017. Impact Investing: Challenges of Impact Measuring. *Goodwin Law*. May. https://www.goodwinlaw.com/-/media/files/publications/attorney-articles/2017/hagedorn-impact-investing-challenges-of-impact-mea.pdf.

Frameworks for Impact Measurement

ICMA: Working Toward a Harmonized Framework for Impact Reporting for Social Bonds

Recognizing both the difficulty and importance of developing a harmonized framework for impact reporting, the ICMA in June 2019 published a set of guidelines for this purpose. It identifies the core principles for reporting on impact as:

(i)   Issuers should put in place a formal internal process for tracking proceeds.
(ii)   Issuers should report on the use of social bond proceeds and on expected social impacts at least annually.
(iii)   Issuers should identify the social project categories to which proceeds have been allocated.
(iv)   Issuers should identify the target populations of the project.
(v)   Issuers should report the output, outcome, and/or impact of projects financed by social bond proceeds, either on a project or portfolio basis, throughout the life of the bond.
(vi)   The impact report should illustrate the expected social impact made possible as a result of projects financed by the social bond.

ICMA also provided specific recommendations for issuers in the following areas: partial eligibility, impact indicators and methodology, share of financing and reporting, life of project impact, assumptions and ex-post verification, reporting period, and disbursement reporting. The report contains a summary template for reporting on social portfolios and projects (Table 4).

Mapping to the Sustainable Development Goals

Even before the pandemic, Asia and the Pacific was not on track to achieve the SDGs by the target date of 2030; the pandemic has paused and likely reversed progress toward these goals. In Southeast Asia, for example, the UN reports that despite strong economic growth before the crisis the region was "beset by numerous challenges including high inequality, low social protection, a large informal sector, and a regression in peace, justice, and robust institutions."[25]

The UN Secretary-General underlines four critical areas for ensuring that recovery from COVID-19 leads to a more sustainable and inclusive future for Southeast Asia:

(i)   tackling inequality in income, health care, and social protection, which will require short-term stimulus as well as long-term, structural reforms;
(ii)   bridging the digital divide so that people and communities are not left behind in an ever-more-connected world;
(iii)   greening the economy to reduce overdependence on coal and other industries of the past, and to create future jobs; and
(iv)   upholding human rights, protecting civic space, and promoting transparency.[26]

Social bond issuers often choose to map their activities to the SDGs. Promulgated in 2015, the SDGs set out the UN's development agenda through 2030. The 17 goals include (i) zero poverty and zero hunger,

---

[25] UN News. 2020. COVID-19: UN Chief Outlines Path to Sustainable, Inclusive Recovery in SE Asia. 30 July. https://news.un.org/en/story/2020/07/1069221.

[26] L. Aquino-Hagedorn and S. Doran. 2017. Impact Investing: Challenges of Impact Measuring. *Goodwin Law*. May. https://www.goodwinlaw.com/-/media/files/publications/attorney-articles/2017/hagedorn-impact-investing-challenges-of-impact-mea.pdf.

Table 4: International Capital Market Association Social Bond Principles Impact Measurement in Practice

Approach	Process	Example	Notes
ICMA SBP	Communicate quantitative and qualitative metrics; address specific issue(s) and target population(s).	East Nippon Expressway Bond in Japan (2020) received third-party evaluation of its social objectives that confirms its alignment with the SBP.	Emphasizes communication and information transparency
Mapping to SDGs	Identify specific SDGs that the bond's proceeds will be used to address.	Shriram Transport Finance Company Bond in India (2020) aligns with SDGs 8 and 10.	In non-high-income Asia, employment generation is the most common use of proceeds.
GIIN IRIS+	Draws on the Catalog of Metrics and standard social and environmental performance metrics for impact investors	Nuveen Affordable Housing Portfolio (over $250 million in assets under management): Outcome targets include increased residential stability, increased resources available after housing payments, improvement in housing quality, and decreased environmental harm	Most valuable for start-up equity investors, especially social enterprises in developing markets
Development Impact Bonds and Social Impact Bonds	Target pre-agreed output and outcome metrics; investor is repaid only after independent evaluator affirms achievement of these metrics	Educate Girls (India, 2015–2018) achieved 160% of the total learning outcomes target and 116% of the total enrollment target for girls in the Rajasthan project	Negotiation of metrics is a lengthy and complex process, usually including government, an intermediary, a social service provider organization, and others.

GIIN = Global Impact Investing Network, ICMA = International Capital Market Association, SBP = Social Bond Principles, SDG = Sustainable Development Goal.
Sources: ICMA Social Bond Principles. 2019. *Working Towards a Harmonized Framework for Impact Reporting in Social Bonds.* https://www.icmagroup.org/assets/documents/Regulatory/Green-Bonds/June-2019/Framework-for-Social-Bond-Reporting-Final-06-2019-100619.pdf; IRIS+Use Case: Nuveen. https://documents.nuveen.com/documents/global/default.aspx?uniqueId=952d59c0-c60f-4d21-bc47-6af0448c0cc2.

(ii) measures to diminish climate change and develop new green technologies, (iii) increased wages and strengthened safety nets around the world, and (iv) improved transparency in public sector revenue management. With many investors looking to comprehensively and quantitatively link their portfolios to the SDGs, while seeking communicating these efforts in a clear and standardized way to clients, issuers and secondary opinion providers often map the bonds' use of proceeds to SDGs in their social bond frameworks. Such mappings, whether open market standards or internal frameworks, are a necessary albeit imperfect way of tying the government and policy-maker-focused SDGs to for-profit commercial investments (Figure 13).

Figure 13: Prevalence of Issuer Social (and Sustainability) Bond Frameworks
That Reference Specific SDGs from 2017–2020, Based on Count of Frameworks

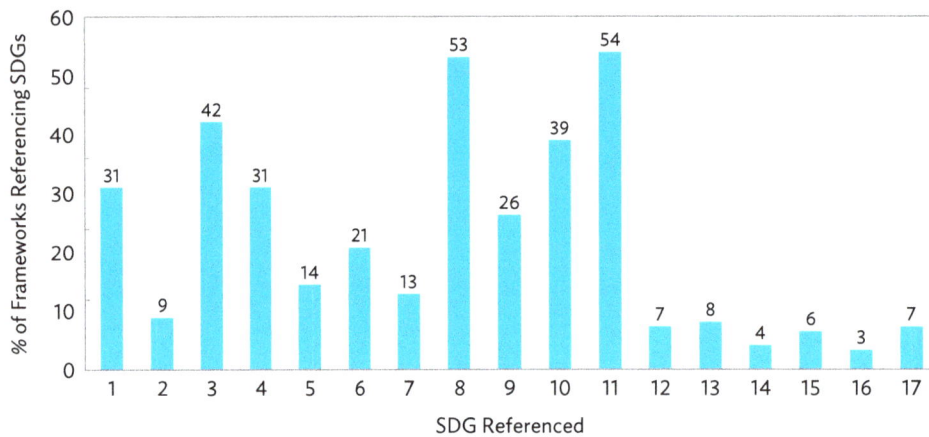

SDG = Sustainable Development Goal.

Note: Totals do not sum to 100% due to overlapping categories.

Sources: Authors' calculations of the percentage of social and sustainability bond frameworks referencing specific SDG targets, based on text-mining analysis of 126 distinct issuer social and sustainability bond frameworks and reviewer second opinions.

We also estimated the USD-equivalent notional allocations by SDG for the social bonds in our database using the same method used for determining notional allocations to SBP project categories and types (Figure 14). From 2017 to 2020, the most allocated SDGs by social bond issuance were SDG 8 (Decent Work and Economic Growth) with a 19% share of allocated USD-equivalent notional, SDG 11 (Sustainable Cities and Communities) with 18%, and SDG 1 (No Poverty) with 17%. SDGs 8, 10 (Reduced Inequalities), and 11 were by far the most targeted SDGs in terms of social bonds issued in non-high-income Asian economies. Finally, we estimate that only 11% of social bond issuance by USD-equivalent notional (excluding social bonds issues under the European Commission's Support to Mitigate Unemployment Risks in an Emergency program) from 2017 to 2020 were allocated to SDG 3 (Good Health and Well-Being), and almost none were allocated in non-high-income economies (Figure 15).

IRIS+

IRIS+ is a system developed by the Global Impact Investing Network for "impact investors to measure, manage, and optimize their impact."[27] Its key features are listed below:

(i) core metrics sets to increase data clarity and comparability;
(ii) thematic taxonomy based on generally accepted impact categories and impact themes;
(iii) updated IRIS catalog of metrics, a generally accepted source of standard social and environmental performance metrics used by leading impact investors;
(iv) curated resources and practical guidance to support day-to-day impact, management, and measurement implementation;
(v) alignment with the SDGs; and
(vi) alignment with other major frameworks and conventions.

[27] Global Impact Investing Network. 2020. Iris+ 2-Pager. https://s3.amazonaws.com/giin-web-assets/iris/assets/files/IRIS_2-Pager.pdf.

Figure 14: Percentage Share of ICMA-Compliant Global Social Bond Issuance Allocation by SDGs, 2017–2020 (USD-equivalent notional, estimated)

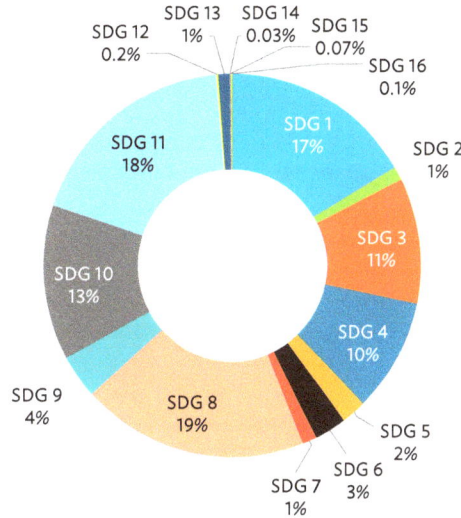

ICMA = International Capital Market Association, SDG = Sustainable Development Goal, USD = United States dollar.

Note: The data do not include European Commission social bonds.

Sources: Authors' calculations based on review of Bloomberg data, issuer social bond frameworks, and reviewer Second Party Opinions.

Figure 15: Percentage Share of ICMA-Compliant Global Social Bond Issuance Allocation by SDGs for Select Asian and Non-Asian Countries, Grouped by Income Level, 2017–2020

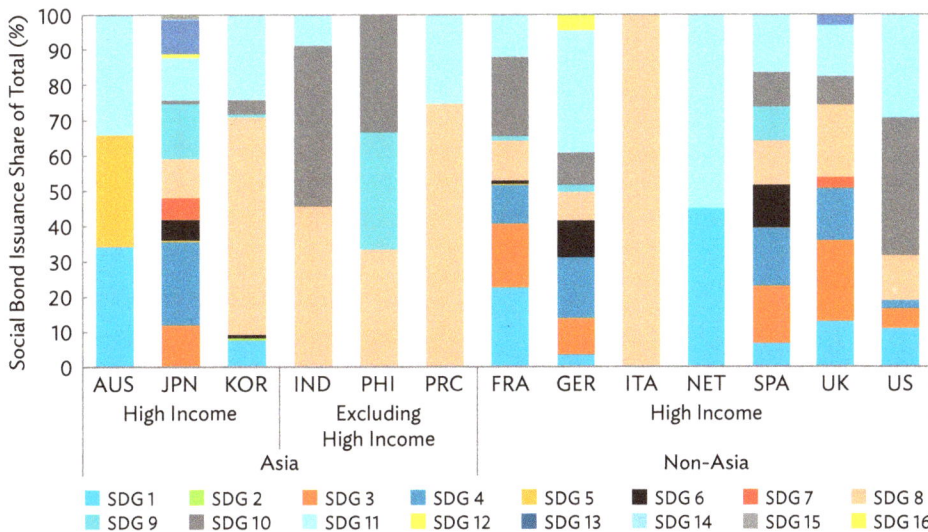

AUS = Australia, FRA = France, GER = Germany, ICMA = International Capital Market Association, IND = India, ITA = Italy, JPN = Japan, KOR = Republic of Korea, NET = Netherlands, PHI = Philippines, PRC = People's Republic of China, SDG = Sustainable Development Goal, SPA = Spain, UK = United Kingdom, US = United States.

Sources: Authors' calculations based on review of Bloomberg data, issuer social bond frameworks, and reviewer Second Party Opinions.

Box 11: Impact Measurement Case Study—ANA Holdings Social Bond

In May 2019, ANA Holdings issued a JPY5 billion ($47 million equivalent) social bond in Japan to finance renovation of airport facilities, facilities and websites for universal services for passengers (services that are easy to use for people with disabilities or elderly people), and renovation of facilities and equipment for universal support for employees. This bond had a well-thought-out framework for impact measurement.

The overall impact of the project was defined as respecting the diversity of ANA's passengers and employees and contributing to the realization of an inclusive society for all. Its evaluation metrics included several output indicators:

(i)   functions (outlines) of the website when the universal compliance renovation was completed,
(ii) number of airports where universal facilities and equipment renovations have been completed, and
(iii) number of office buildings where universal works and equipment renovations have been completed.

Outcomes will be measured by the number of passengers with disabilities who use ANA flights and the employment ratio of persons with disabilities.

The bond was aligned with Sustainable Development Goals 10 and 11. Under the International Capital Market Association's Social Bond Principles framework, it was mapped to

(i) improved access to essential services for the disabled and elderly (i.e., socially vulnerable populations), and
(ii) socioeconomic empowerment for the disabled and LGBT (i.e., socially vulnerable populations).

Source: Japan Credit Rating Agency. 2019. Social Bond Evaluation News Release. 16 May. https://www.jcr.co.jp/download/cf0efc6a2e88df78e765eecca5fcc7cce876cc6ef592decc56/19d0140en.pdf.

IRIS+ appears more relevant to start-up and early-stage funding for impact investing projects, especially social enterprises in developing markets, than to the listed bond market of which social bonds are a part and where investors tend to dislike complexity (Box 11). It is valuable, though, in its "promotion of transparency, credibility, and accountability in the use of impact data for decision making across the impact investment industry."[28]

Sustainability Accounting Standards Board

The Sustainability Accounting Standards Board "sets sustainability disclosure standards that are industry-specific and tied to the concept of materiality to investors."[29] This helps investors by promoting company disclosure of data on standardized ESG and other sustainability issues that is "comparable, consistent, and financially material."[30] While the Sustainability Accounting Standards Board is mainly focused on the materiality of ESG factors rather than impact itself and may be considered to have a more equity market-centric perspective, it is doing valuable work for bond investors in Asia by providing a market-focused ESG framework as a starting point.

Impact Measurement Project

The Impact Measurement Project, which describes itself as a "forum for building global consensus on how to measure and manage impacts," brings together more than 2,000 enterprises and investors to determine best practices in defining and measuring impact. It has developed a consensus among these organizations that impact can be measured across five dimensions:

---

[28] Footnote 27.
[29] Sustainability Accounting Standards Board. https://www.sasb.org/about/.
[30] Footnote 29.

(i)   **What** tells us what outcome the enterprise is contributing to, whether it is positive or negative, and how important the outcome is to stakeholders.

(ii)   **Who** tells us which stakeholders are experiencing the outcome and how underserved they are in relation to the outcome.

(iii)   **How much** tells us how many stakeholders experienced the outcome, what degree of change they experienced, and how long they experienced the outcome for.

(iv)   **Contribution** tells us whether an enterprise's and/or investor's efforts resulted in outcomes that were likely better than what would have occurred otherwise.

(v)   **Risk** tells us the likelihood that impact will be different than expected.[31]

Learning from Impact Bonds

The example of social impact bonds (SIBs) and DIBs is relevant to impact measurement since they are based on the principle of pay-for-success and so impact measurement is critical to their formulation. However, SIBs and DIBs are not useful for meeting large-scale and near-term social needs in Asia due to their small size, complexity, and long lead time. Furthermore, they are not really fixed-income securities at all. However, impact management and assessment is central to these instruments since investors get paid only if the projects meet certain agreed-upon impact metrics. Thus, they can offer some insights into the issue areas addressed and the measurement methodologies used for performance-based instruments.

Impact Areas

Per the Brookings Global Impact Bonds Database, from 2010 to 2020, 206 SIBs and DIBs were contracted in 35 economies across six sectors, representing $434 million in capital raised. Most of these deals were in a small number of economies: the United Kingdom (69), the US (26), the Netherlands (15), Portugal (13), and Australia (10). Only 18 SIBs and DIBs have been contracted in low- and middle-income economies. These instruments have focused largely on two issue areas: employment and social welfare (Figure 16).[32]

It is unclear whether these issue areas reflect investor interest, relative ease of outcomes measurement, government priorities, or availability of investable social service organizations.

Impact Measurement in SIBs and DIBs

Outcome metrics for each SIB and DIB are essentially bespoke; metrics are not consistent and comparable across categories because the instruments fund different types of social programs and aim to achieve different goals. Outcomes tracked thus far include such diverse categories as family reunification, stable housing, and employment. A little more than half tie their results to outcomes, while others measure a combination of outputs and outcomes (Table 5). (Outputs typically track the completion of an activity, like a training program; outcomes measure the impact of the program on the individual.)

---

[31] Impact Management Project. Impact Management Norms. https://impactmanagementproject.com/impact-management/impact-management-norms/ (accessed 20 October 2020).

[32] E. Gustafsson-Wright. 2020. What Is the Size and Scope of the Impact Bonds Market? *Brookings Impact Bonds Brief.* https://www.brookings.edu/wp-content/uploads/2020/09/Impact_Bonds-Brief_1-FINAL-1.pdf.

Figure 16: Impact Areas Addressed by Social and Development Impact Bonds, 2010–2020

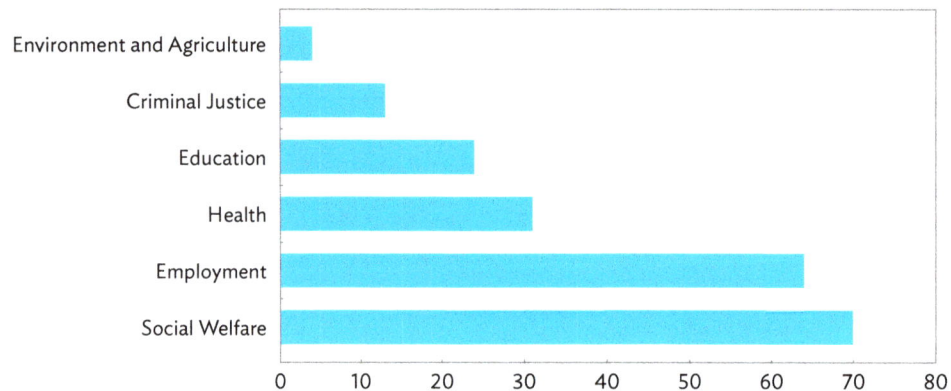

Source: Brookings Institution.

Table 5: Types of Metrics Used for Impact Bonds as of July 2020

Contracted Impact Bonds Total	Outcomes	Outcomes and Outputs	Outputs	Data Not Available
194	109	49	5	31

Source: Brookings Institution.

A sampling of the criteria for evaluation includes

(i)   paying investors for each student who did not require unnecessary special education, based on avoided costs to the state;

(ii)   paying investors based on improvements in the recidivism rate of men released from prison as compared to a control group; and

(iii)   paying investors based on the number of people employed or in school or training, the number of families preserved or reunited, and the number of people in stable housing.

These outcomes, however, sidestep two critical questions. First, the evaluation process only considers the value of the social intervention being financed, not the value added by the impact bond mechanism itself—a problem of additionality. Second, it is impossible to know whether the outcomes are sustainable beyond the length of the impact bond period (usually 3–7 years).[33]

---

[33] E. Gustafsson-Wright, M. Massey, and S. Osborne. 2020. Are Impact Bonds Delivering Outcomes and Paying Out Returns? *Brookings.* https://www.brookings.edu/wp-content/uploads/2020/09/Are-impact-bonds-delivering-outcomes-and-paying-out-returns-FINAL-2.pdf.

Conclusions—Optimizing Impact in the COVID-19 Era and Beyond

4

Based on our novel dataset of estimated social bond allocations by SBP project category and type, we draw several conclusions about the state of the social bond market and its development during the COVID-19 pandemic.

The first finding is that, overall, the growth in global social bond issuance in 2020 by SBP project type was mainly driven by the large rise in allocated funding for education and training, SME finance, and crisis-related unemployment alleviation, with the latter being a new SBP project type created in 2020. Project types such as health and digital access, while ostensibly also relevant to the COVID-19 pandemic, saw lower rates of growth than might have been expected. One possible explanation for this is that the spending needs for acute pandemic response for consumables such as personal protective equipment, medicines, and vaccine procurement are more practical to fund out of general-purpose budgets than long-term debt capital financing. It is also possible that long-term capital spending on medical facilities and equipment requires more time and will be finalized for increased issuance later. It is clear, however, that a major function of the social bond market during the pandemic so far has been to rapidly raise capital to support struggling SMEs and the unemployed with skills and job training in addition to direct assistance.

The second finding is that SME finance was far more dominant in Asian social bond issuance during 2020 than in the rest of the world. We estimate that social bonds issued in the region in 2020 had a relatively large focus on the economic fallout of the pandemic, particularly on SME financing, which was the top project type by far. In contrast, social bond markets outside of Asia and the Pacific (primarily high-income European economies) raised the largest allocation for projects related to education and training, as well as crisis-related unemployment alleviation spending. While SME finance was the single largest project allocation type in Asia and the Pacific in 2020 with over $9.4 billion equivalent in estimated allocations, this same type only raised $5.0 billion equivalent in the rest of the world (excluding supranational issuance), where it was only the fifth-largest project type in 2020. This may be due to the relative greater number of social bond frameworks in non-Asian economies that designate education and training for use of proceeds (46% vs 25%), reflecting differences in regional social safety nets and socioeconomic structure.

Breaking down this regional view further by income level, we find that the allocations to SBP project types in high-income Asia in 2020 were nearly 39% SME finance, 19% access to transport, and 17% affordable housing, with less than 6% allocated to health-related projects or assets. Aside from allocations to access to transport and the relatively low weight of education and training, high-income Asia's pattern of issuance is not particularly different from social bond issuance patterns in non-Asian high-income economies, especially when considering that SME finance and crisis-related unemployment alleviation are conceptually very similar.

On the other hand, non-high-income Asia shows a distinct issuance pattern compared to non-high-income economies outside of the region (although the relative lack of issuance from such economies makes comparison difficult.) We estimate that nearly 100% of non-high-income Asian social bond issuance in 2020 was allocated for SME finance, whereas outside of Asia and the Pacific such issuance was more focused on meeting basic needs, particularly affordable housing, education and training, in addition to health-related spending.

Asia and the Pacific is deeply important to the world economy, with the potential to act as a growth driver for other regions to recover from the COVID-19 crisis. For the past 2 years, the Emerging Market Private Equity Association's investor survey has ranked Southeast Asia as the world's most attractive market for investment, citing its strong macroeconomic growth, solid civil infrastructure, government support, and growing pipeline of investable businesses. Asia and the Pacific's emerging markets dominate the survey, with India and the People's Republic of China in the top three positions.[34] Asian economies were the ones struck first by the virus, and they are now poised to restart their economies sooner than the rest of the world. But in order to fulfill this potential, Asia and the Pacific will need to build back better by directing public and private funds to the right issues and in the right ways.

[34] V. Erogbogbo and A. Khanna. 2020. SME Investing With a Gender Lens: The Key to COVID-19 Recovery in Emerging Markets. *Next Billion*. 20 August. https://nextbillion.net/sme-investing-gender-COVID-emerging-markets/.

The Way Forward

5

The question is, then, how to help developing economies in Asia and the Pacific catch up to where they were and start progressing again; that is, how to ensure that the temporary reversals of the COVID-19 era do not become permanent socioeconomic scarring.[35] In a recent report, Moody's Investor Services stated that the pandemic will intensify stakeholders' focus on ESG factors and suggested that three areas will dominate this shift: (i) institutional preparedness for high-impact global risks (i.e., resilience), (ii) health-care access, and (iii) economic inequality.[36]

This suggests a growing demand for social bonds, which can address these high-priority areas. At the same time, it is challenging for policy makers, issuers, and investors to fully determine which issue areas should be addressed through social bond financing. Without standardized impact measurement methodologies, market participants' ability to compare projects is limited; and with so many high-priority needs, hard decisions will be necessary. As a general rule, issuers will disclose whatever they can track by themselves with relative ease.

One challenge to high-quality impact reporting is a lack of data. Here, governments and development banks can play an important role in stimulating the sector. Banks can implement internal systems for tracking and monitoring loan portfolios, while updating lending guidelines to incorporate ESG data along with impact measurements. Regulators can then collect information for the entire banking sector. Governments and development banks can formulate relevant data sets for evaluation; governments and corporates should adapt to disclosing data in an open and digitized form. We know that investors shy away from complexity, so harmonization and standardization of data can expand the social bond market, while improving liquidity, which is highly valued by investors. In addition, by increasing disclosure of ESG-focused activities by government and corporate borrowers, improved impact reporting will improve governance, which is also highly valued by investors and other stakeholders.

On the other hand, given the differences between social values and preferences in different communities, true harmonization of outcomes measurement may be neither desirable nor possible on a global scale. This may create some market segmentation and reduce market efficiency, but it also provides an opportunity to tailor impact investments based on the differing value systems and real needs of different regions.

Finally, corporate treasurers sometimes view social bonds narrowly as a vehicle for reducing funding costs. If this reduction is not apparent, they may not bother with the additional due diligence, reporting, and coordination needed for such instruments. But this mindset is changing; as more investors view ESG assessment as a basic foundation for investment, companies will increasingly face higher funding costs if they do not demonstrate a commitment to ESG as well.

---

[35] Footnote 4.
[36] E. Johansson. 2020. August 17). Shift to Multi-Stakeholder Model to Spur Sustainable Bonds. *Expert Investor*. 17 August. https://expertinvestoreurope.com/shift-to-multi-stakeholder-model-to-spur-sustainable-bonds/.

The good news is that social bonds have proven to be valuable instruments for directing private capital to socioeconomic priorities. From resilience to SME support, gender equity to health care, social bonds will be an essential tool for financing the work needed for developing Asia to build back better.

Note on Methodology

This note will explain our applied methodology for estimating the "allocated SBP project categories and types" as well as "allocated SDG target funding" used in this analysis. First, we reviewed the social bond framework (or the social bond project categories and project types of the sustainability bond framework if no social bond framework was present) for every global International Capital Market Association (ICMA)-compliant social bond issuer in our database, based on issuances from 2016 to 2020. We then compiled a standardized database of which Social Bond Principles (SBP)-compliant project categories and types were specifically identified in the issuer's own framework or second opinion report. These included use of proceeds from the original SBP 2018 definition covering health, affordable housing, and small and medium-sized enterprises (SMEs) and microfinance, as well as the updated SBP 2020 project categories such as crisis-related unemployment alleviation. This process was also completed for the Sustainable Development Goal (SDG) targets identified in the issuers' social and sustainability bond framework. Since each individual framework can and often does address multiple and overlapping SBP project categories and types (and SDG targets), we calculated the share of each as 1/n, where n was the number of project categories and types or SDGs identified in the framework. For example, if the issuers' ICMA-compliant social bond framework specified SME finance and education and training projects for the use of proceeds, then we allocated 50% to each type for every one of that issuers' social bonds issued under the same framework. We used this data to estimate the allocation of each of the issuers' social bonds to distinct SBP project categories, project types, and SDGs in a globally consistent and comparable manner. We caveat that this method may not capture the exact breakdown of project funding per social bond, as the use of proceeds is not likely to be allocated equally across project types and may even shift over time (such as increasing allocations to health-related projects during the coronavirus disease pandemic).

www.ingramcontent.com/pod-product-compliance
Lightning Source LLC
Chambersburg PA
CBHW042035220326
41599CB00045BA/7425